The People of
IRELAND
1600-1699

Part Four

IRELAND IN THE REIGN OF JAMES I.

The People of
IRELAND
1600-1699

Part Four

by
David Dobson

CLEARFIELD

Copyright © 2014
by David Dobson
All Rights Reserved

Printed for Clearfield Company by
Genealogical Publishing Company
Baltimore, Maryland
2014

ISBN 978-0-8063-5702-7

INTRODUCTION

People of Irish origin face a challenging task when they attempt to trace their early roots. The church records, such as registers of baptism, marriage, and burial, which are so essential to research elsewhere in the British Isles, as they identify virtually everyone at all levels of society, are far from comprehensive. This is particularly true for the seventeenth century when the Irish diaspora, partly to continental Europe but increasingly to the Americas, began to become significant. The predominant religion was, and still is Catholicism but there are very few church registers extant prior to the mid-eighteenth century. The earliest ones, though incomplete, exist for the town of Wexford from 1671, while those of the cities of Waterford and Galway date from the 1680s. There are a few Church of Ireland registers of baptism and marriage dating from the early seventeenth century, such as certain Dublin parishes, but most date from around 1770. The vast majority of Presbyterian churches were, and remain, located in the north of Ireland. Their earliest registers date from the 1670s. On the other hand the Society of Friends [Quakers] has maintained excellent records dating from the mid-seventeenth century. Family historians seeking their Irish roots of the seventeenth century are therefore faced with using a wide range of alternative source material, both published and manuscript. Most of these have been identified by genealogists, such as Margaret Dickson Falley in her *Irish and Scotch-Irish Ancestral Research*, and more recently William J. Roulston in his *Researching Scots-Irish Ancestors*. However much of this is in original material in Ireland not accessible to the ordinary researcher, while some of the publications can only be located in a few specialist libraries, such as The National Library of Ireland in Dublin, or the Public Record Office of Northern Ireland in Belfast. The series *The People of Ireland, 1600-1699* attempts to bring much relatively obscure material together in concise source books. It is based largely on primary sources such as published government records together with references found in Irish, British, and continental European sources.

The most important published sources used in this compilation are the *Calendar of Patent Rolls, Ireland* and various collections of documents in private hands published by the *Historical Manuscript Commission*. The main archives used was *The National Archives* in

London where the records of the *High Court of the Admiralty of England* proved particularly interesting.

This source book can be used to identify the locations where particular surnames or families can be found during the seventeenth century. The aim is to provide information on ordinary people throughout Ireland, with the exception of people of Scottish origin who have been dealt with in my *Scots-Irish Links, 1575-1725* series. Consequently the people listed are predominately of native Irish and immigrant English origin, as well as a handful of Dutch or Flemish origin. The source citations generally should be followed up as the sources should provide supplementary data so essential when writing up family histories.

David Dobson

Dundee, Scotland

2014

THE PEOPLE OF IRELAND, 1600-1699, PART FOUR

ABLIN, ISAACK, from Caen, Normandy, a grant of naturalisation in Ireland, 18 January 1656. [Patent Roll, Commonwealth, 1.3/29]

ACRIGG, MILES, in the parish of Clones, Barony of Clankelly, County Fermanagh, was killed by rebels in 1641. [PRONI.MIC.8.2]

ADSHEAD, THOMAS, was granted a pass to go to Ireland, 13 March 1656. [Cal.SPDom.1655.579]

AILWARD, PIERS, Vice Admiral of Waterford, 1617. [Carew mss. 1617.178]

ALEN, MATHEW, of Palmerstown, died 14 July 1645. [Palmerstown MI]

ALLAN, PATRICK, a Roman Catholic in St Woolstans, County Kildare, licensed to bear a sword, a case of pistols, and a gun, 30 March 1705. [HMC.Ormond.ii.475]

ALLEN, ROBERT, Clerk of the Peace in County Cavan, 9 May 1628. [CPRI]

ALLAND, HENRY, a merchant in Waterford, 1678. [LRS.36.53]

ANCKETELL, OLIVER, of Ancketill Grove, died at Armagh, buried 28 June 1666. [St Patrick's Church of Ireland, Monaghan, MI]

ANDREWS, JOHN, born in Catherlogh, a cordwinder, took the Oath of Allegiance and Supremacy to King Charles II, on 29 April 1671.

ANDREWS, WILLIAM, Mayor of Cork, 1705. [TNA.SP34.8.97]

ANNESLEY, Sir FRANCIS, with 1000 acres in Wexford, 1616. [Carew mss.1616.168]; was created Baron of Mountnorris in Ireland, 8 February 1629. [CPRI]

AP HUGH, AMBROSE, in County Louth, 1611. [Carew mss]

AP HUGH, RICE, who was convicted of the murder of James Booth was pardoned but sentenced to be burnt in the hand, 23 June 1631. [CPRI]

ARCHBOLD, WILLIAM, a baker in Dublin city, took the Oath of Allegiance and Supremacy to King Charles II, on 12 July 1665.

THE PEOPLE OF IRELAND, 1600-1699, PART FOUR

ARCHDALE, EDWARD, was granted land in County Fermanagh to be known as the manors of Archdale and Dromra, 22 December 1629. [CPRI]

ARCHDALE, JOHN, a gentleman with 1000 acres in the precinct of Colinkernan, County Fermanagh, 1611. [Carew mss.1617.130]

ARCHDEACON, KATHERINE, born in 1685, a spinster from Bramhall, County Kilkenny, indented for 4 years' service in America in Liverpool, 1704. [LRO]

ARCHDEACON, WILLIAM, born 1685 in Waterford, settled as a merchant in Ostend, Flanders, in 1705, and later in Bruges, Flanders. [SAA.IB.360]

ARCHER, JOHN, deposition, 12 March 1642. [TCD.ms818. 42]

ARCHER, MATHEW, officer for the assize of bread and beer in Waterford, 1617. [Carew mss.1617.178]

ARMELY, OWEN, born in Clanrichard, a tailor, took the Oath of Allegiance and Supremacy to King Charles II, on 12 September 1668.

ARTAN, EDWARD, master of the Thomas of Wexford, captured by Parliamentary forces when bound from Wexford to St Malo, France, in 1649. [TNA.HCA.15.2]

ARTHUR, JOHN, a Roman Catholic in Caberagh, County Dublin, licensed to bear a sword, a case of pistols, and a gun, 30 March 1705. [HMC.Ormond.ii.475]

ASHBORNEHAM, Sir JOHN, with 2000 acres in the precinct of Clogher, County Tyrone, 1611. [Carew mss. 1611.130]

ASHTON, MICHAEL, drew lands in the Barony of Upper Iveagh, County Down, 1659. [CSPI.1903.343]

ASTON, THOMAS, in the parish of Clones, Barony of Clankelly, County Fermanagh, was killed by rebels in 1641. [PRONI.MIC.8.2]

ATHEY, NICHOLAS, resident of Galway, 26 October 1652. [HHG, appx.xxxii]

THE PEOPLE OF IRELAND, 1600-1699, PART FOUR

AUDLEY, FERNANDO, with 2000 acres in the precinct of Omey, County Tyrone, 1611. [Carew mss. 1611.130]

AUDLEY, Sir MERVYN, with 2000 acres in the precinct of Omey, County Tyrone, 1611. [Carew mss. 1611.130]

AUSTIN, EDMUND, drew lands in the Barony of Deece, County Meath, 1659. [CSPI.1903.343]

AYER, JOHN, armed with a sword and pike, in Barony of Loughty, County Cavan, 1630. [BL.Add.MS.4770]

AYLMER, CATHERINE, a spinster in Ballrath, County Meath, will, 1710. [DRD]

AYLMER, Colonel GEORGE, a Roman Catholic in Lyons, County Kildare, licensed to bear a sword, a case of pistols, and a gun, 30 March 1705. [HMC.Ormond.ii.475]

BAGOTT, MARK, late of Mount Arran, County Caterlogh, now of Dublin, a Roman Catholic licensed to bear a sword, a case of pistols, and a gun, 30 March 1705. [HMC.Ormond.ii.475]

BAGGOTT, NICHOLAS, in County Kildare, was pardoned in Dublin on 23 July 1608. [HMC.Hastings.iv.32]

BAGNOLL, ARTHUR, of Newry, County Down, 1611. [Carew mss]

BAILY, JOHN, born in Trallex, County Kerry, a carpenter, took the Oath of Allegiance and Supremacy to King Charles II, on 1 June 1667.

BAILY, ['Bely'], WILLIAM JOHN, from Ireland, married Annetie Negenduysent in Rotterdam, Holland, on 7 August 1695. [Scots Kirk register in Rotterdam]

BALDON, LAURENCE, porter of the gates of Waterford, 1617. [Carew mss.1617.178]

BALLARD, THOMAS, of Cuckfield, Sussex, drew lands in the Barony of Deece, County Meath, 1659. [CSPI; 1903.216/343]

BANCLINCH, THOMAS, a merchant in Galway, 1678. [LRS.36.15]

THE PEOPLE OF IRELAND, 1600-1699, PART FOUR

BARBER, CHARLES, from Kilkenny, indented for 5 years' service in Virginia, sailed aboard the <u>Eleanor of Liverpool</u> in 1698. [LRO]

BARE-WALTERTON, SAMUEL, granted a pass to go to Ireland 16 May 1656. [CalSPDom.1655.582]

BARKER, WILLIAM, a merchant in London, drew lands in the Barony of Upper Iveagh, County Down, 1659. [CSPI; 1903.343]

BARKLEY, Sir NORRIS, with 2000 acres in the precinct of Liffer, County Donegal, 1611. [Carew mss. 1611.130]

BARLOR, CHARITY, from Kilkenny, indented for 5 years' service in America, sailed from Liverpool, England, in 1698. [LRO]

BARLOWE, Dr RANDOLPH, Dean of Christ Church, was appointed Archbishop of Tuam on 2 April 1629. [CPRI]

BARNARD, RICHARD, of Lewes, Sussex, drew lands in the Barony of Deece, County Meath, 1659. [CSPI; 1903.343]

BARNES, BRIAN, in Barony of Loughty, County Cavan, 1630. [BL.Add.MS.4770]

BARNES, Sir WILLIAM, with 1500 acres in the precinct of Liffer, County Donegal, 1611. [Carew mss. 1611.130]

BARNEWELL, JOHN, commonly called Lord Trembleston, a Roman Catholic licensed to bear a sword, 30 March 1705. [HMC.Ormond.ii.475]

BARNEWELL, MATTHEW, son and heir of Edward Barnewell late of Moylagh, County Meath, and ward of Richard Fitzgerald of the city of Dublin, 8 March 1632. [CPRI]

BARNEWALL, NICHOLAS, in Dublin City, a Roman Catholic licensed to bear a sword, a case of pistols, and a gun, 30 March 1705. [HMC.Ormond.ii.475]

BARNEWALL, PATRICK, son and heir of John Barnewall late of Angor, County Meath, 9 August 1632. [CPRI]

BARRON, GEOFFREY, son and heir of Laurence Barron late of Clonmel, 26 February 1628. [CPRI]

THE PEOPLE OF IRELAND, 1600-1699, PART FOUR

BARRON, GEORGE, 'sworn measurer' of Waterford, 1617. [Carew mss. 1617.178]

BARRON, JOHN, searcher of Waterford, 1617. [Carew mss.1617.178]

BARON, LAURENCE, master of the privateer John Baptist of Waterford, 1648. [TNA.HCA.30.855.378; 13.61.209]

BARRY, DANIEL, born in County Cork 1649, brown hair, enlisted as a horseman of the King's Guard in 1676. [HMC.Ormonde.ii.237]

BARRY, GERROTT FITZJAMES, late of Ballytrasney, County Cork, 5 December 1631. [CPRI]

BARRY, JOHN, of Ballicloghie, 19 November 1632. [CPRI]

BARRY, LAURENCE, born in County Cork 1646, enlisted as a horseman of the King's Guard in 1667. [HMC.Ormonde.ii.237]

BARTON, THOMAS, with 1000 acres in the precinct of Colinkernan, County Fermanagh, 1611. [Carew mss.1617.130]

BARTHOW, THOMAS, armed with a sword and pike, in Barony of Loughty, County Cavan, 1630. [BL.Add.MS.4770]

BARWICK, THOMAS, drew lands in the south east quarter of the Barony of Lecale, County Down, 1659. [CSPI; 1903.342]

BATEMAN, ANNE, and sisters, drew lands in the north east quarter of the Barony of Lecale, County Down, 1659. [CSPI; 1903.342]

BATH, PATRICK, son and heir of Robert Bath of Colps, County Meath, 29 December 1628. [CPRI]

BATH, PETER, a prisoner sentenced to death, was banished to Barbados, 31 July 1654. [IC.ii.522]

BAYLY, DAVID, keeper of the 'corn and kett' in Waterford, 1617. [Carew mss.1617.178]

BEACH, ..., master of the privateer Michael of Wexford, 1648. [TNA.HCA.13.249]

THE PEOPLE OF IRELAND, 1600-1699, PART FOUR

BEACHIE, WILLIAM, master of the Dolphin of Wexford, captured by Parliamentary forces in 1647. [TNA.HCA.15.2]

BEAGHAN, EDMOND, was appointed Summonister of the Court of Exchequer on 3 September 1629. [CPRI]

BEDELL, WILLIAM, Provost of Trinity College, was consecrated Bishop of Kilmore and Ardagh on 21 May 1629. [CPRI]

BEE, JOHN, son and heir of James Bee an alderman late of the city of Dublin, 16 January 1629. [CPRI]

BEEWATER, NICHOLAS, in Baltimore, County Cork, was pardoned in Dublin on 18 January 1608. [HMC. Hastings.iv.29]

BEGG, ROGER, was granted a pass to go to Ireland 16 May 1656. [CalSPDom.1655.582]

BEGGE, WALTER, son and heir of Nicholas Begge late of Borranstown alias Sillfocke, County Dublin, 20 September 1628. [CPRI]

BEGGELLY, GEORGE, born 1656, died 5 May 1716. [Tullaght MI]

BEHAES, or DEHAES, GABRIEL, from Antwerp, Flanders, a grant of denization in Ireland, 10 April 1605. [IPR]

BELL, THOMAS, a merchant in Belfast, trading with Denmark, 1677. [TNA.SP63.338.33]

BELLASYSE, Sir HENRY, late Governor of the town and garrison of Galway, 1705. [TNA.SP3.21.260]

BELLEW, PATRICK, son and heir of Richard Bellew of Verdanstown, County Louth, 21 November 1628. [CPRI]

BELLEW, Sir PATRICK, a Roman Catholic licensed to bear a sword, a case of pistols, and a gun, 30 March 1705. [HMC.Ormond.ii.475]

BELLEW, Lord RICHARD, a Roman Catholic licensed to bear a sword, a case of pistols, and a gun, 30 March 1705. [HMC.Ormond.ii.475]

BENNET, ROBERT, a yeoman in County Cork, 'a tory, thief or robber', to be apprehended and tried, 1692. [HMC.Ormonde.ii.449]

THE PEOPLE OF IRELAND, 1600-1699, PART FOUR

BENNETT, THOMAS, in Baltimore, County Cork, was pardoned in Dublin on 18 January 1608. [HMC. Hastings.iv.29]

BENSON, PETER, was granted land in the precinct of Liffer, Barony of Raphoe, County Donegal, 11 July 1629. [CPRI]

BERKELEY, EDWARD, born in Limerick 1636, grey hair, enlisted as a horseman of the King's Guard in 1676. [HMC.Ormonde.ii.237]

BERMINGHAM, JOHN, son and heir of Amie Delahoid, 20 July 1631. [CPRI]

BERMINGHAM, JOHN, a Roman Catholic prisoner in Dublin, to be released on 3condition that he moved to Connaught, 6 February 1657. [IC.ii.918]

BERMINGHAM, WALTER, son and heir of William Bermingham in County Kildare, 21 September 1629. [CPRI]

BERRES, ROBERT, master of the Poote of Londonderry, 1614. [UPB.64]

BERRIDGE, ZABULON, a merchant, churchwarden of Christchurch, Waterford, 1617. [Carew.1617.178]

BERRIE, DAVID, from Cork, married Ann Sprie a widow in the Reformed Presbyterian Church in Rotterdam, Holland, on 8 November 1702.

BEST, JOHN, master of the Allen of Waterford, captured by Parliamentary forces when bound from Waterford to Bristol and St Malo, France, 1649. [TNA.HCA13.250.II]

BETAGH, RICHARD, son and heir of James Betagh late of Killyhane, County Galway, 19 July 1631. [CPRI]

BETSON, JOHN, master of the Carvel of Coleraine, and of the Blessing of Coleraine, 1614. [UPB.10/70]

BEXFORD, RICHARD, resident of Galway, 11 April 1652. [HHG, appx.xxxii]

BIGG, MATHEW, drew lands in the Barony of Deece, County Meath, 1659. [CSPI; 1903.343]

BIGGOE, PHILLIP, from France, in Birr, King's County, a grant of denization in Ireland, 10 June 1637. [IPR]

BIGNALL, PHEBE, armed with a sword and snaphance, in Barony of Loughty, County Cavan, 1630. [BL.Add.MS.4770]

BILLEN, ADAM, master of the Dolphin of Cork, from Ireland to San Sebastian, Spain, 1705. [TNA.SP44.392.53]

BILLINGTON, Dame DEBORAH, a widow in Dublin, will, 1708. [DRD]

BIRD, CHARLES, from Bandon, Cork, a mariner aboard the Centurion, probate 1699. [PCC]

BIRD, Captain, an English Protestant, in Galway town, 1657. [HHG.appx.XXXVI]

BISCOE, JOSEPH, drew lands in the Barony of Upper Iveagh, County Down, 1659. [CSPI; 1903.343]

BLACK, JOHN, from Ireland, married Maetje Thyssen from Rotterdam, Holland, there on 23 September 1635.

BLACK, JOHN, from Ireland, married Plasant Parker from England in the Reformed Church, Rotterdam, Holland, on 26 January 1642.

BLACKLY, MATTHEW, jr., born 1677, died 28 November 1703, son of Matthew Blackley sr. who died 26 November 1704. [St Tigernach's Church of Ireland, Clones, MI]

BLAKE, HENRY, a merchant in Galway, 29 February 1632. [CPRI]

BLAKE, JOHN, Recorder of Galway, 26 October 1652. [HHG, appx.xxxii]

BLEALICKE, THOMAS, master of the Sunday of Ardglass, 1615. [UPB. 102]

BLENERHASSETT, Sir EDWARD, with 2000 acres in the precinct of Clancally, County Fermanagh, 1611. [Carew mss. 1611.130]

BLENERHASSETT, JOHN, in Ballyseedy, County Kerry, husband of Margaret, will, 1709. [DRD]

THE PEOPLE OF IRELAND, 1600-1699, PART FOUR

BLENERHASSETT, THOMAS, with 2000 acres in the precinct of Clancally, County Fermanagh, 1611. [Carew mss. 1611.130]

BLUNDELL, FRANCIS, with 1000 acres in Wexford, 1616. [Carew mss. 1616.168]

BLUNT, ..., with 2000 acres in the precinct of Omey, County Tyrone, 1611. [Carew mss. 1611.130]

BODKIN, DOMINICK, master of the Solomon of Waterford, captured by Parliamentary forces in 1644. [TNA.HCA.3.230]

BODKIN, ROBERT, master of the Harrington of Dublin, from Galway to San Sebastian, Spain, 1705. [TNA.SP44.390.367]

BOELL, WILLIAM, from Antwerp in Brabant, a grant of denization in Ireland, 11 June 1607. [IPR]

BOGGAS, ROBERT, a gentleman with 1000 acres in the precinct of Colinkernan, County Fermanagh, 1611. [Carew mss.1617.130]

BOGHELLY, DANIEL, a yeoman in County Cork, 'a tory, thief or robber', to be apprehended and tried, 1692. [HMC.Ormonde.ii.449]

BOGHELY, DERMOD, a yeoman in County Cork, 'a tory, thief or robber', to be apprehended and tried, 1692. [HMC.Ormonde.ii.449]

BOISSEAU, PETER, master of the Providence of Cork, from Cork to San Sebastian, Spain, 1705. [TNA.SP44.392.51]

BOR, CHRISTIAN, a gentleman from the Netherlands, a grant of denization in Ireland, 14 May 1618. [IPR]

BOR, JOHN, a gentleman from the Netherlands, a grant of denization in Ireland, 14 May 1618. [IPR]

BORRON, NICHOLAS, born in Dublin 1647, brown hair, enlisted as a horseman of the King's Guard in 1663. [HMC.Ormonde.ii.237]

BOSSGEL, PATRICK, an Irish soldier, a thief banished from Leiden, Holland, 9 November 1621. [PL.54]

BOUYE, JOHN, born in Thouneux, Languedoc, France, son of Jean Bouye, residing in the parish of St Michael, Dublin, a grant of naturalization, 1678. [Patent Roll, 30 Car ii.20]

BOWDEN, EGIDIUS or GILES, from Germany, a grant of denization in Ireland, 17 July 1634. [IPR]

BOY, WILLIAM, master of the Mary of Dublin, captured by Parliamentary forces when bound from Dublin to Chester, England, in 1644. [TNA.HCA.13.62]

BOYLAN, BRYAN, born 1653, died 10 February 1733. [Killeevan MI]

BOYLAND, CARMOCK, born 1602, a mariner from Carrickfergus, County Antrim, a witness before the High Court of the Admiralty of England in April 1639. [TNA.HCA.55/2]

BOYLE, CHARLOTTE, born in Paris, France, daughter of Francis, Viscount Shannon, brother to the Earl of Cork, a grant of naturalisation, 1661. [Patent Roll, 14 Car ii.1]

BOYLE, RICHARD, born in France, son and heir of Lord Viscount Shannon, a grant of naturalisation in England, 1675. [Patent Roll, 27 Car ii.3]

BOYLE, WILLIAM, master of the Betty of Cork, from Ireland to Bilbao, Spain, and return, 1705. [TNA.SP44.392.67]

BOYTON, EDMUND, of Casshall, County Cork, was pardoned in Dublin on 12 December 1607. [HMC.Hastings.iv]

BRADY, LUKE, was licenced to hold markets in the town of Tomgreany, County Clare, 29 February 1631. [CPRI]

BRAG, THOMAS, in the Barony of Loughty, County Cavan, 1630. [BL.Add.MS.4770]

BRASELOGH, TIRLOGH OGE MCTIRLOGH, a native who was granted land in the Precinct of Oriel, 1611. [Carew mss]

BRAYE, ROBERT, a merchant aboard the Speedwell of Strangford from Portaferry to Wyre, 1615. [UPB.102]

THE PEOPLE OF IRELAND, 1600-1699, PART FOUR

BREMINGHAM, EDMOND, son and heir of James Bremingham late of Ballivollane, County West Meath, 6 December 1631. [CPRI]

BREMINGHAM, JOHN, son and heir of Walter Bremingham late of Carrick, County Kildare, 8 March 1631. [CPRI]

BREMINGHAM, PATRICK, son and heir of William Bremingham of Corbally, County Meath, 7 March 1628. [CPRI]

BREMINGHAM, PIERCE, son and heir of John Bremingham late of Garresher, County Kildare, 11 March 1632. [CPRI]

BRETT, IGNATIUS, master of the privateer Patrick of Wexford, 1649. [TNA.HCA.15.2]

BREWSTER, Mr NATHANIEL, minister of Christ Church in Dublin, 1656. [IC.ii.848]

BRIAN, JAMES, son and heir of Richard Brian late of Lissevolan, County West Meath, 28 June 1632. [CPRI]

BRIAN, JOHN, son and heir of James Brian late of Whitewall, County Kilkenny, 24 March 1631. [CPRI]

BRICE, CHRISTOPHER, was granted 1189 acres in County West Meath and 466 acres in King's County on 1 May 1629. [CPRI]

BRIGGS, MILES, a merchant tailor in London, drew lands in the Barony of Deece, County Meath, 1659. [CSPI; 1903.343]

BRODER, RICHARD, in County Galway, 'a tory, thief or robber', to be apprehended and tried, 1692. [HMC.Ormonde.ii.449]

BROOKES, HENRY, was armed with a snaphance, in Barony of Loughty, County Cavan, 1630. [BL.Add.MS.4770]

BROOKE, HENRY, in County Fermanagh, a petition, 1705. [TNA.SP63.366.23-26; SP44.240.315-316]

BROOKES, JOHN, in Barony of Loughty, County Cavan, 1630. [BL.Add.MS.4770]

BROOKS, MARTIN, master of the Greyhound of Londonderry, 1614. [UPB.4]

THE PEOPLE OF IRELAND, 1600-1699, PART FOUR

BROWKER, THOMAS, of Newnham, Northamptonshire, drew lands in the Barony of Upper Iveagh, County Down, 1659. [CSPI; 1903.343]

BROWNE, ADAM, master of the privateer Trinity of Waterford, 1649. [TNA.HCA.34.4.74]

BROWN, Mr ALEXANDER, died 28 April 1703, his wife Sarah, born 1654, died 2 February 1710, their son Joseph Brown, born 1689, died 1 January 1713, [Tullynish MI]

BROWN, ARTHUR, born 1699, son of Reverend John B. Brown in Drogheda, an Anglican minister sent to Providence, New England, in 1729. [EMA.17]

BROWN, CHRISTOPHER, born 1585 in Clontarf by Dublin, a seaman aboard the Lyon of Fairlie, a witness before the High Court of the Admiralty of England in April 1640. [TNA.HCA.55.607; 55.586]

BROWN, DANIEL, of Jobstown, died in February 1700. [Tullaght MI]

BROWNE, DOMINICK, resident of Galway, 11 April 1652. [HHG, appx.xxxii]

BROWNE, IGNATIUS, born in Galway, a pewterer, took the Oath of Allegiance and Supremacy to King Charles II, on 12 October 1670.

BROWNE, JOHN, a merchant, churchwarden of Ladychurch, Waterford, 1617. [Carew.1617.178]

BROWN, JOHN, surveyor of Waterford, 1617. [Carew mss.1617.178]

BROWNE, JOHN, born in Tinihealy, County Wicklow, took the Oath of Allegiance and Supremacy to King Charles II, on 21 October 1667.

BROWNE, JOHN, born in Dublin, a merchant, took the Oath of Allegiance and Supremacy to King Charles II, on 18 September 1672.

BROWN, Colonel JOHN, in Westport, County Mayo, a Roman Catholic licensed to bear a sword, a case of pistols, and a gun, 30 March 1705. [HMC.Ormond.ii.475]

BROWNE, MARCUS, resident of Galway, 11 April 1652. [HHG, appx.xxxii]

BROWN, RICHARD, born 1605 in Cork, a merchant, a witness before the High Court of the Admiralty of England in October 1627. [TNA.HCA. 13.46/388/313]

BROWN, ROBERT, examination, 26 December 1653. [TCD. ms818. 208]

BROWNE, STEPHEN, a Catholic, in Galway town, 1640. [HHG.appx.XXXVI]

BROWNE, THOMAS, a Catholic, in Galway town, 1640. [HHG.appx.XXXVI]

BROWNLOW, WILLIAM, a gentleman, with 2000 acres in the precinct of Oneylan, County Armagh, 1611. [Carew mss.1611.130]

BRYAN, Captain CHRISTOPHER O., in Enisman, County Clare, a Roman Catholic licensed to bear a sword, a case of pistols, and a gun, 30 March 1705. [HMC.Ormond.ii.475]

BRYAN, JAMES, late of Kilkenny, now in Jenkinstown, County Kilkenny, a Roman Catholic licensed to bear a sword, a case of pistols, and a gun, 30 March 1705. [HMC.Ormond.ii.475]

BRYAN, RICHARD, of Longwood, County Kildare, 1611. [Carew mss]

BRYANT, THOMAS, born in Youghal, Captain of the Elizabeth of Youghal, a witness before the High Court of the Admiralty of England in October 1627. [TNA.HCA13.46/378] [APCE.1627.205]

BRYVER, FRANCIS, son and heir of James Bryver late of Waterford, 3 March 1629. [CPRI]

BULKELEY, Sir RICHARD, bt., of Old Bawn, County Dublin, will, 1710. [DRD]

BULLER, JAMES, Presbyterian, a burgess of Belfast from 1690 to 1703. [BMF]

BULLER, PHILIP, in Athlone, probate 1699. [PCC]

BURK, Lieutenant Colonel JOHN, in Milford, County Galway, a Roman Catholic licensed to bear a sword, a case of pistols, and a gun, 30 March 1705. [HMC.Ormond.ii.475]

BURK, Colonel THOMAS, in Portumna, County Galway, a Roman Catholic licensed to bear a sword, a case of pistols, and a gun, 30 March 1705. [HMC.Ormond.ii.475]

BURK, Sir ULICK, in Glinske, County Galway, a Roman Catholic licensed to bear a sword, a case of pistols, and a gun, 30 March 1705. [HMC.Ormond.ii.475]

BURMAN, WILLIAM, in Yorkshire, drew lands in the north east quarter of the Barony of Lecale, County Down, 1659. [CSPI; 1903.342]

BURNE, PHILIP, born 1702 in Ireland, an indentured servant in King William County, Virginia, who absconded in 1752. [VaGaz.18.6.1752]

BURNELL, HENRY, in Dublin, 1611. [Carew mss]

BURY, GEORGE, vicar of Cahir in the Diocese of Lismore, accused of adultery in 1698-1700, a petition dated 25 November 1705. [TNA.SP44.242.36-40]

BUTLER, GEORGE, in Barony of Loughty, County Cavan, 1630. [BL.Add.MS.4770]

BUTLER, JAMES, born 1651, late Duke of Ormond, died in Avignon, France, in 1745. [SM.7.543]

BUTLER, Captain JAMES, was killed at the battle of Aghrim, his widow Sarah petitioned King William in 1697. [CTP.XLIV.59]

BUTLER, Captain JAMES, born 1663, related to the late Duke of Ormond, died in Lisbon, Portugal, on 13 July 1766. [SM.28.389]

BUTLER, Colonel JAMES, in Kilveolugher, County Tipperary, a Roman Catholic licensed to bear a sword, a case of pistols, and a gun, 30 March 1705. [HMC.Ormond.ii.475]

BUTLER, JOAN, widow of George Bagnall late of Dunliken, County Carlow, was licenced to marry whom she pleases, on payment of a fine of £10, 26 November 1631. [CPRI]

THE PEOPLE OF IRELAND, 1600-1699, PART FOUR

BUTLER, JOHN, was transported by Captain Bryan Fitzpatrick for service under the King of Sweden, 1630. [APCE.1630.1304]

BUTLER, JOHN, in West Court, County Kilkenny, a Roman Catholic licensed to bear a sword, 30 March 1705. [HMC.Ormond.ii.475]

BUTLER, PEIRCE, grandchild and heir of Peirce Butler of Callan, and ward of Philip Butler, 21 May 1631. [CPRI]

BUTLER, RICHARD, son and heir of Nicholas Butler late of Ballyknavine, County Waterford, 20 February 1631. [CPRI]

BUTLER, RICHARD, son and heir of Peirse Butler of Castle Connor, County Kilkenny, 10 December 1631. [CPRI]

BUTLER, RICHARD, son and heir of William Butler late of Oughtragh, County Tipperary, 13 December 1632.[CPRI]

BUTLER, Lieutenant Colonel RICKARD, in Gortamadin, County Galway, a Roman Catholic licensed to bear a sword, a case of pistols, and a gun, 30 March 1705. [HMC.Ormond.ii.475]

BUTLER, STEPHEN, a gentleman with 2000 acres in the precinct of Loughte, County Cavan, 1611. [Carew mss.1611.130]

BUTLER, THEOBALD, son and heir of Edward Butler late of Ardmaile, County Tipperary, 30 October 1628. [CPRI]

BUTLER, THEOBALD, in Dublin City, a Roman Catholic licensed to bear a sword, a case of pistols, and a gun, 30 March 1705. [HMC.Ormond.ii.475]

BUTLER, THOMAS, was transported by Captain Bryan Fitzpatrick for service under the King of Sweden, 1630. [APCE.1630.1304]

BUTLER, Colonel THOMAS, in Kilcash, County Tipperary, a Roman Catholic licensed to bear a sword, a case of pistols, and a gun, 30 March 1705. [HMC.Ormond.ii.475]

BUTLER, Colonel WALTER, in Memphin, County Wexford, a Roman Catholic licensed to bear a sword, a case of pistols, and a gun, 30 March 1705. [HMC.Ormond.ii.475]

THE PEOPLE OF IRELAND, 1600-1699, PART FOUR

BUTLER, Colonel, born 1674, 'for many years in Imperial Service and a relation of the late Duke of Ormond', died in Barcelona, Spain, on 16 January 1769. [SM.31.54]

BYRNE, DANIEL, in Dublin City, a Roman Catholic licensed to bear a sword, a case of pistols, and a gun, 30 March 1705. [HMC.Ormond.ii.475]

BYRNE, Sir GREGORY, in Killene, Queen's County, a Roman Catholic licensed to bear a sword, a case of pistols, and a gun, 30 March 1705. [HMC.Ormond.ii.475]

BYRNE, HUE, was transported by Captain Bryan Fitzpatrick for service under the King of Sweden, 1630. [APCE.1630.1304]

BYRNE, PATRICK, born 1654, died 16 May 1701. [St Mola's Church of Ireland, Magheracloone MI]

CADE, JOHN, born in County Cork 1654, enlisted as a horseman of the King's Guard in 1675. [HMC.Ormonde.ii.237]

CADMORE, SAMUEL, a merchant in Waterford, 1680. [LRS.36.152/163]

CAGE, ROBERT, Controller of the port of Wexford before July 1629. [CPRI]

CAGLY, BRYAN, born 1664, died 1 February 1714. [Killeevan MI]

CALVERT, ROBERT, a gentleman with 1000 acres in the precinct of Colinkernan, County Fermanagh, 1611. [Carew mss.1617.130]

CAMPION, WILLIAM, master of the True Amity of Dublin, from Youghal to Bilbao, Spain, and return, 1705. [TNA.SP44.390.322]

CAN, BRIAN, born 1621 in Galway, a mariner of an Irish man o'war, a witness before the High Court of the Admiralty of England in May 1649. [TNA.HCA13.61/502]

CANARAUGH, JAMES, born 1629 in Wexford, a sailor aboard the man o'war Catherine of Wexford, a witness before the High Court of the Admiralty of England in May 1649.[TNA.HCA13.61.502]

CARBERRY, JOHN, in Kilbride, County Dublin, a Roman Catholic licensed to bear a sword, 30 March 1705. [HMC.Ormond.ii.475]

CAREW, ANTHONIE, born 1629 in Waterford, a merchant in Ostend, Flanders, around 1660. Burgomaster there from 1667. [RAB, registers Brugse vrije nrs 17121/17122, and 17163]

CAREW, ROGER, of Lismore, a juror at Blackfriars, County Waterford, 5 September 1617. [Carew mss.1617.184]

CAREW, THOMASINA, widow of Sir George Carew, a pensioner, 11 May 1631. [CPRI]

CARLETON, GEORGE, Clerk of the Crown and Hanaper in Chancery of Ireland, 11 January 1631. [CPRI]

CARRILL, CHARLES, was granted a pass to go to Ireland on 13 March 1656. [Cal.SPDom.1655.579]

CARROLL, Sir JAMES, with 1000 acres in Wexford, 1616. [Carew mss. 1616.168]

CARRINE, DANIELL, was transported by Captain Bryan Fitzpatrick for service under the King of Sweden, 1630. [APCE.1630.1304]

CARROLL, Sir JAMES, in Dublin, probate 1660 PCC. [TNA]

CARTIE, DANIEL, son of Teige McDonnell Cartie late of Disert, County Cork, and ward of Barnaby Tottenham, 6 March 1631. [CPRI]

CARTIE, DERMOT, son and heir of John McFynin Cartie late of Aghirishmore, County Cork, 23 May 1631. [CPRI]

CARTIE, FYNNAN, son and heir of Dermot Mcnogher Cartie late of Maddane, County Cork, 3 December 1632. [CPRI]

CARTY, MICHAEL, master of the Unity of Youghall, from Ireland to Bilbao, Spain, 1705. [TNA.SP44.390.375]

CARTY, OWEN MCCALLAGHAN, son and heir of Callaghan McCartie late of Dromlegagh, 5 December 1631. [CPRI]

CASE, ROBERT, born 1591 in Bunratty, County Clare, a seaman, a witness before the High Court of the Admiralty of England in May 1642. [TNA.HCA13.58.77/20]

CASTLEHAVEN, Lord JAMES, a Roman Catholic licensed to bear a sword, 30 March 1705. [HMC.Ormond.ii.475]

CEYDOR, LUDVIK, master of the Peter of Wexford, captured by Parliamentary forces when bound from France to Wexford, in 1640s. [TNA.HCA.34.1.377]

CHADICK, GEORGE, in Barony of Loughty, County Cavan, 1630. [BL.Add.MS.4770]

CHADS, HENRY, a merchant in Belfast, probate 29 June 1711. [PRONI.T559/15/133]

CHAMBERS, JAMES, of Tullyrean, born 1683, died 8 November 1757. [Seapatrick MI]

CHAPLIN, ANDREW, vicar of Kilconry and Killmalliere in the Diocese of Killaloe, 8 July 1631. [CPRI]

CHARLTON, GEORGE, in Wexford, deposition, 24 January 1642. [TCD.ms818.57]

CHEEVERS, DAVID, master of the Mayflower of Waterford, captured by Parliamentary forces when bound from Plymouth, England, to Cork in 1642. [TNA.HCA.13.58.60]

CHESTON, RICHARD, in Barony of Loughty, County Cavan, 1630. [BL.Add.MS.4770]

CHICHESTER, CHARLES, of the Church of Ireland, a gentleman and a burgess of Belfast from 1697 to 1701. [BMF]

CHICHESTER, JAMES, of the Church of Ireland, a gentleman and a burgess of Belfast from 1698 to 1721. [BMF]

CHILD, JOHN, in Baltimore, County Cork, was pardoned in Dublin on 18 January 1608. [HMC. Hastings.iv.29]

CHUBB, SAMPSON, of Munster, Ireland, probate 1657 PCC. [TNA]

CHUTE, THOMAS, was appointed Chancellor of the cathedral of St Brandon in the Diocese of Ardfert, 16 May 1631. [CPRI]

CLARE, Sir HENRY, with 1500 acres in the precinct of Liffer, County Donegal, 1611. [Carew mss. 1611.130]

CLARK, PHILIP, of Tallow, a juror at Blackfriars, County Waterford, 5 September 1617. [Carew mss.1617.184]

CLEARE, ROBERT, was pardoned in Dublin on 23 July 1608. [HMC.Hastings.iv.32]

CLEAVER, JOHN, born in County Monaghan 1645, enlisted as a horseman of the King's Guard in 1668. [HMC.Ormonde.ii.237]

CLEERE, WALTER, Mayor of Waterford, 1617. [Carew mss.1617.184]

CLEMENTS, ANN, born 1683, a spinster from Dublin, indented for 4 years' service in America, sailed from Liverpool in 1704. [LRO]

CLINCH, SIMON, in College, County Dublin, a Roman Catholic licensed to bear a sword, a case of pistols, and a gun, 30 March 1705. [HMC.Ormond.ii.475]

CLINTON, CHARLES, was appointed a vicar in the Diocese of Cashel and Emly on 5 August 1629. [CPRI]

CLINTON, MARY, daughter and heiress of Nicholas Clinton a merchant in Dublin City, 20 March 1631. [CPRI]

CLOTHIER, HERCULES, born 1608 in Kinsale, a seaman aboard the Elisabeth and Anne, a witness before the High Court of the Admiralty of England in June 1644. [TNA.HCA13.52.291/292]

CONNALL, WILLIAM, born 1593, a merchant from Waterford, a witness before the High Court of the Admiralty of England in June 1624. [TNA.HCA13.44.327]

CONNELL, JAMES, born 1604, a mariner aboard the Hercules, a witness before the High Court of the Admiralty of England in November 1644. [TNA.HCA13.47.403]

COACH, Captain, with 1500 acres in the precinct of Liffer, County Donegal, 1611. [Carew mss. 1611.130]

COAN, THADY, died 1681. [Ballyshannon MI]

THE PEOPLE OF IRELAND, 1600-1699, PART FOUR

COANE, THAD, born 1658, died 29 October 1723. [Ballyshannon Abbey MI]

COD, NICHOLAS, son and heir of Martin Cod of Castletown, County Wexford, 13 May 1631. [CPRI]

CODIE, JOHN, was transported by Captain Bryan Fitzpatrick for service under the King of Sweden, 1630. [APCE.1630.1304]

COFFY, EDMOND, son and heir of Thomas Coffy late of Ballinhina, County West Meath, and ward of John Coffy, 20 July 1631. [CPRI]

COGAN, PETER, a merchant in Coleraine, 1615. [UPB.87]

COLCLOUGH, ADAM, was granted the manor of Tintern in County Wexford, on 19 June 1628. [CPRI]

COLCLOGH, CAESAR, in Rossgarland, County Wexford, a Roman Catholic licensed to bear a sword, a case of pistols, and a gun, 30 March 1705. [HMC.Ormond.ii.475]

COLCLOGH, Colonel DUDLEY, in Moyhery, County Wexford, a Roman Catholic licensed to bear a sword, a case of pistols, and a gun, 30 March 1705. [HMC.Ormond.ii.475]

COLE, Sir WILLIAM, of Innis Killyn, County Fermanagh, probate 1657 PCC. [TNA]

COLEN, TERENCE, died 21 May 1713. [Ballyshannon Abbey MI]

COLLEY, CHRISTOPHER, born in Kildare, enlisted as a horseman of the King's Guard in 1674. [HMC.Ormonde.ii.237]

COLLEY, GERRALD, born in Dublin, a gentleman, took the Oath of Allegiance and Supremacy to King Charles II, on 28 August 1667.

COLLINS, GEORGE, master of the St Patrick of Waterford, captured by Parliamentary forces when bound from Waterford to Bilbao, Spain, in 1646. [TNA.HCA.13.62/248]

COMERFORD, GERALD, son and heir of Foulke Comerford late of Inchcolehane, County Kilkenny, 16 February 1632. [CPRI]

THE PEOPLE OF IRELAND, 1600-1699, PART FOUR

COMERFORD, RICHARD, harbinger of Waterford, 1617. [Carew mss.1617.178]

COMYN, DAVID, son and heir of Nicholas Comyn alderman of Limerick, 10 March 1628. [CPRI]

CONDON, JAMES, son and heir of Walter Condon late of Aghlishe, County Cork, 23 June 1632. [CPRI]

CONDON, JOHN, son and heir of Richard Condon late of Carrig Inonry, County Cork, 23 February 1628. [CPRI]

CONNELLY, OWEN, examination, 22 October 1641. [TCD.ms809.13]

CONNELLY ,......, born 1676, died near Edinderry, Ireland, in 1794. 'He remembered the landing of King William and the Battle of the Boyne'. [SM.56.412]

CONNER, CORNELIUS, a Roman Catholic priest, bound for Ireland aboard the Nostra Dama de Le Croisic in 1645. [TNA.HCA.13.60]

CONNOR, BRYAN RABATH, in County Roscommon, 'a tory, thief or robber', to be apprehended and tried, 1692. [HMC.Ormonde.ii.449]

CONROY, ..., Collector at Kinsale, a report, 1705. [TNA.SP63.366.69]

CONTENT, JOSEPH, master of the privateer St Peter of Waterford, 1648. [TNA.HCA.15.2]

COOKE, EDWARD, a yeoman in Drogheda, was pardoned, 19 July 1631. [CPRI]

COOKE, Sir RICHARD, with 1000 acres in Wexford, 1616. [Carew mss. 1616.168]

COOK, THOMAS, a merchant in Cork, trading with the West Indies, 1686. [SPAWI.1686.910]

COPE, RICHARD, was granted land in the Barony of O'Nealan, County Armagh, and in the barony of Clogher, County Tyrone, 14 October 1629. [CPRI]

COPE, RICHARD, born in County Armagh, enlisted as a horseman of the King's Guard in 1673. [HMC.Ormonde.ii.237]

CORNELISON, JOHN, of Galway, took the Oath of Allegiance and Supremacy to King Charles II, on 2 August 1670.

CORNELISSON, ADRIAN, from Holland, a grant of denization in Ireland, 22 December 1617. [IPR]

CORNELISSON, WYBRANS OCKER, from Holland, a grant of denization in Ireland, 22 December 1617. [IPR]

CORNWALL, Sir THOMAS, with 2000 acres in the precinct of Liffer, County Donegal, 1611. [Carew mss. 1611.130]

CORRIGAN, CHARLES JOHNSON, in Waterford, a deed, 1694. [GAR.ONA.1053.6/202]

CORRIGAN, FREDERICK JOHNSON, in Waterford, a deed, 1694. [GAR.ONA.1053.6/202]

COSBY, ALEXANDER, son and heir of Richard Cosby late of Stradbally, Queen's County, 18 May 1632. [CPRI]

COSBY, ELISABETH, widow of Richard Cosby late of Stradbally, was pardoned for marrying Barnaby Dunne without a licence, 14 March 1632. [CPRI]

COTTINGHAM, SEBASTIAN, in the parish of Clones, Barony of Clankelly, County Fermanagh, was killed by rebels in 1641. [PRONI.MIC.8.2]

COUGHLAN, JOHN, in Bandonbridge, County Cork, husband of Dorothy Gookin, will, 1709. [DRD]

COULSON, JOHN, drew lands in the north west quarter of the Barony of Lecale, County Down, 1659. [CSPI; 1903.342]

COURSE, JOHN, born 1640, died in Calvintown, County Kildare, on 18 August 1752. 'He was born in Languedoc, France, bred a Protestant, served in the French Army, later in Dutch service, to Ireland under the Duke of Schomberg, enlisted under King William, fought against King James, then took up farming.' [SM.14.415]

THE PEOPLE OF IRELAND, 1600-1699, PART FOUR

COURSEY, JAMES, master of the <u>Adventure of Waterford</u>, from Waterford to Bilbao, Spain, in 1705. [TNA.SP44.390.393]

COWLEY, Sir GEORGE, in King's County, 1611. [Carew mss]

COWLEY, THOMAS, born 1621, a seaman from Dublin, a witness before the High Court of the Admiralty of England in April 1646. [TNA.HCA13.60.538/374]

COWLTY, CHRISTOPHER, master of the <u>Trinity of Ardglass</u>, 1615. [UPB.98]

COX, JUDITH, born in Moscow, Muscovy, wife of Maurice Keating of Noroghmore, County Kildare, a grant of naturalization in Ireland,1654.

COX, NICHOLAS, of the city of Kilkenny, 27 October 1632. [CPRI]

CRAGH, DONNOGH, was transported by Captain Bryan Fitzpatrick for service under the King of Sweden, 1630. [APCE.1630.1304]

CRAMER, BALTHAZAR, from Geesin, Upper Germany, a grant of denization in Ireland, 29 January 1620. [IPR]

CRAWDOCK, JOHN, in Barony of Loughty, County Cavan, 1630. [BL.Add.MS.4770]

CRAWLEY, MARGARET, born in Dundalk in 1688, 'had been abroad in all Queen Anne's wars as keeper of a suttling booth in the camps. She had, for many years past, let out lodgings to poor people, and is said to have died worth near £2000 the greatest part of which she has left to a blacksmith. She had been married to nine husbands, but never had any issue', 1766. [SM.27.391]

CREAGH, THOMAS, master of the <u>Mary of Dublin,</u> a dogger, from Limerick to Bilbao, Spain, and return, 1705. [TNA.SP44.393.16]

CREED, ARTHUR, born 1600, a Customs Officer in Ross, Ireland, a witness before the High Court of the Admiralty of England in May 1642. [TNA.HCA13.58/85]

CREELEY, PATRICK, master of the Griffin of Drogheda trading between Coleraine and Spain, 1615. [UPB.84]

CRESSIE, Sir ROBERT, was licenced to hold markets in Conge, County Mayo, 9 July 1631. [CPRI]

CREELEY, PATRICK, master of the Griffin of Drogheda trading between Coleraine and Spain, 1615. [UPB.84]

CROCKER, HUGH, of Copayryn, a juror at Blackfriars, County Waterford, 5 September 1617. [Carew mss.1617.184]

CROFTON, ANTHONY, from County Sligo, a mariner aboard HMS Lynne, probate, 1700. [PCC]

CROMWELL, EDWARD, born 1559, Baron of Okkham, died 24 September 1607. [Down Cathedral MI]

CROMWELL, EDWARD, was pardoned in Dublin on 23 July 1608. [HMC.Hastings.iv.32]

CROMWELL, OLIVER, son of the Earl of Ardglas and grandson of Edward Cromwell [above], died 19 October 1668. [Down Cathedral MI]

CROOK, ANDREW, printer to the King, Ormonde Quay, Dublin, 1695. [NLI]

CROOKE, THOMAS, in Baltimore, County Cork, was pardoned in Dublin on 18 January 1608. [HMC. Hastings.iv.29]

CROOKE, Sir THOMAS, born 1578, from Baltimore, County Cork, a witness before the High Court of the Admiralty of England in April 1629. [TNA.HCA13.48/241]

CRUMPHOUT, HUBERT, born 1616, a merchant in Dublin, a witness before the High Court of the Admiralty of England in September 1645. [TNA.HCA13.60/204]

CRUISE, PATRICK, in Tatrath, County Meath, a Roman Catholic licensed to bear a sword, a case of pistols, and a gun, 30 March 1705. [HMC.Ormond.ii.475]

CRY, THEOBALD, sergeant of the kitchen in Waterford, 1617. [Carew mss.1617.178]

CUFF, ALEXANDER, gentleman, churchwarden of Christchurch, Waterford, 1617. [Carew.1617.178]

CUFF, ALEXANDER, clerk of the Ordnance, constable of the passage, and gunner of Waterford, 1617. [Carew mss.1617.178]

CUFF, WAREHAM, water bailiff of Waterford, 1617. [Carew mss. 1617.178]

CULME, BENJAMIN, Dean of St Patrick's in Dublin, probate 1658 PCC. [TNA]

CUPPAIGE, THOMAS, a gentleman in Lambstown, County Wexford, husband of Elizabeth Cuppaige, will, 1709. [DRD]

CURRAN, DAVID, born 1670, from Dublin, indented for 4 years' service in America, sailed from Liverpool bound for the Chesapeake in 1700. [LRO]

CUSACK, ROBERT, late of Kilcolgan, now of Rathgarr, County Dublin, a Roman Catholic licensed to bear a sword, a case of pistols, and a gun, 30 March 1705. [HMC.Ormond.ii.475]

DALE, Captain DENNIS, an army pensioner in Ireland, a petitioner 1626. [APCE.1626.106]

DALIE, JOHN, born 1596, master of the Unity of Kinsale, 1641-1642, a witness before the High Court of the Admiralty of England in April 1642. [TNA.HCA13.58.1/4-5]

DALLAWAY, JOHN, gentleman in Cashelton, County Kildare, was pardoned in Dublin on 23 July 1608. [HMC.Hastings.iv.32]

DALTON, ROGER, of Knockmoan, a juror at Blackfriars, County Waterford, 5 September 1617. [Carew mss.1617.184]

DAYLEY, DAN, born 1598, pilot aboard the Gift of God of Cork, a witness before the High Court of the Admiralty of England in March 1649. [TNA.HCA13.61.351/2]

DALY, DENNIS, in Dublin City, a Roman Catholic licensed to bear a sword, a case of pistols, and a gun, 30 March 1705. [HMC.Ormond.ii. 475]

DALY, Major EDMOND, in Gortnemuck, King's County, a Roman Catholic licensed to bear a sword, a case of pistols, and a gun, 30 March 1705. [HMC.Ormond.ii.475]

DALY, JOHN, master of the Unity of Cork, captured by Parliamentary forces when bound from St Malo, France to Cork in 1642. [TNA.HCA.13.58.4]

DALY, OWEN, a Roman Catholic priest, bound for Ireland aboard the Nostra Dama de Le Croisic in 1645. [TNA.HCA.13.60]

DAMUCH, CHRISTOFFEL, from Ireland, a hodman, married Maertgen Robbertsdaughter, widow of Willem Adams, in Leiden, Holland, 10 November 1638. [Leiden Marriage Register]

DARCY, JAMES, an alderman of Galway, 26 October 1652. [HHG, appx.xxxii]

DAVID, ROCHE, a Frenchman from Guyene, who settled in Cork before 1698. [TNA.SP34.8.97]

DAVIES, JOHN, of the Church of Ireland, a merchant and a burgess of Belfast from 1642 to 1667. [BMF]

DAVIES, WILLIAM, born 1676, from Belfast, indented for 4 years' service in the American colonies, sailed from Liverpool bound for Montserrat in 1700. [LRO]

DAVIS, Sir JOHN, with 2000 acres in the precinct of Omey, County Tyrone, 1611. [Carew mss. 1611.130]

DAVIS, JONAS, from Cork, indented for 4 years' service in America, sailed from Liverpool in 1698. [LRO]

DAVYS, PAUL, of St Catherine's, County Dublin, was created Viscount Mount Cashell, County Tipperary, on 5 December 1705. [TNA.SP67.3.247-8]

DAWSON, JOSHUA, keeper of the Paper Office in Ireland, 1705. [TNA.SO1.15.352-3]

DAY, JAMES, born 1688, from Dublin, indented for 5 years' service in America, sailed from Liverpool bound for Newfoundland in 1700. [LRO]

DEANE, STEPHEN, a merchant in Galway, 1678. [LRS.36.15.22]

DE COCQUIEL, JACQUES, from Germany, a grant of denization in Ireland, 17 July 1634. [IPR]

DE LA COURT, JAMES, a gentleman of Baniknakan, County Cork, probate, 1700. [PCC]

DE LA HIDE, PATRICK, born 1600, a merchant from Drogheda, a witness before the High Court of the Admiralty of England in September 1623. [TNA.HCA13.44.172]

DE LA HIDE, RICHARD, born 1604, a merchant from Drogheda aboard the Talbott, a witness before the High Court of the Admiralty of England in August 1627. [TNA.HCA13.46.325]

DE LA MARE, JOHN, son and heir of William Delamare late of Rath, County West Meath, 14 March 1628. [CPRI]

DE LAUSSAC, ANTOINE, a French pensioner in Ireland, with his wife Jane, and daughter Marie, 1705. [TNA.SO1.15.327]

DELHUNTY, Colonel LAWRENCE, in Shandagin, County Clare, a Roman Catholic licensed to bear a sword, a case of pistols, and a gun, 30 March 1705. [HMC.Ormond.ii.475]

DE LA MARE, JOHN, in Dublin City, a Roman Catholic licensed to bear a sword, a case of pistols, and a gun, 30 March 1705. [HMC.Ormond.ii.475]

DE LA MARE, Major WALTER, in Dublin City, a Roman Catholic licensed to bear a sword, a case of pistols, and a gun, 30 March 1705. [HMC.Ormond.ii.475]

DE LAUNE, HENRY, from France, a grant of denization in Ireland, 9 January 1628. [IPR]

DE LEON, ABRAHAM, from Endhoven, Brabant, a grant of denization in Ireland, 12 October 1621. [IPR]

DENNIS, STEPHEN, a merchant from France, a grant of denization in Ireland, 28 April 1628. [IPR]

DENNISON, DERRICK, master of the Fortune of Wexford, captured by Parliamentary forces when bound from Wexford to St Lucar, Spain, in 1643. [TNA.HCA.13.58.616]

DENNY, EDWARD, of Traly, County Kerry, husband of Mary, will, 1710. [DRD]

DERRIRO, OWEN, a yeoman in County Cork, 'a tory, thief or robber', to be apprehended and tried, 1692. [HMC.Ormonde.ii.449]

DES MYNIEIRES, LEWIS, born in Amersfoot, Utrecht, Netherlands, a grant of denization in Ireland on 11 December 1655. [Patent Roll, Commonwealth, 1.3]; a merchant, a grant of naturalization 1662. [IPR. 14-15 Car ii]

DE SYMON, JOHN, master of the Nicholas of Galway, captured by Parliamentary forces when bound from Nantes, France to Galway in 1644. [TNA.HCA.13.59.565]

DEVEREUX, JOHN, brother and heir of Alexander Devereux of Moyglass, County Wexford, 5 March 1628. [CPRI]

DEWSBERRY, ADAM, drummer, in Barony of Loughty, County Cavan, 1630. [BL.Add.MS.4770]

DEWSBERRY, JOHN, in Barony of Loughty, County Cavan, 1630. [BL.Add.MS.4770]

DEYNISH, WILLIAM, porter of the gates of Waterford, 1617. [Carew mss.1617.178]

DEYNISH, WILLIAM, keeper of the 'corn and kett' in Waterford, 1617. [Carew mss.1617.178]

DICKSON, JOHN, born 1665, died 7 February 1703. [Loughbrickland MI, Aghaderg]

DILLON, Captain GERALD, in Manning, County Mayo, a Roman Catholic licensed to bear a sword, a case of pistols, and a gun, 30 March 1705. [HMC.Ormond.ii.475]

DILLON, Lord Viscount HENRY, in Costelloe, County Mayo, a Roman Catholic licensed to bear a sword, a case of pistols, and a gun, 30 March 1705. [HMC.Ormond.ii.475]

DILLON, JAMES, born in County Meath 1649, brown hair, enlisted as a horseman of the King's Guard in 1667. [HMC.Ormonde.ii.237]

DILLON, JOHN, a gentleman, with 2000 acres in the precinct of Oneylan, County Armagh, 1611. [Carew mss.1611.130]; was granted lands to be called the manor of Castledillon, 13 August 1629. [CPRI]

DILLON, LUKE, son and heir of George Dillon of Killeighe, County Dublin, 31 December 1628. [CPRI]

DILLON, RICHARD, gentleman and his servant **RICHARD DILLON,** Roman Catholic prisoners in Dublin, to be released on condition that he moved to Connaught, 6 February 1657. [IC.ii.918]

DIXON, JOHN, born in Athlone, County Roscommon, a merchant, took the Oath of Allegiance and Supremacy to King Charles II, on 18 April 1670.

DIXON, RICHARD, armed with a sword and pike, in Barony of Loughty, County Cavan, 1630. [BL.Add.MS.4770]

DOBIN, ROBERT, 'sworn measurer' of Waterford, 1617. [Carew mss. 1617.178]

DOBBIN, WILLIAM, merchant in Carrickfergus, 1615. [UPB.93]

DOBBIN, Captain WILLIAM, born 1650, a merchant in Belfast, died 7 October 1723. [PRONI.T367]

DOCKWRA, Sir THEODORE, Constable of the Fort at Cariestown, Ranelaghs, County Wicklow, 11 March 1629. [CPRI]

DONE, PATRICK, master of the Blessing of God of Killough, 1614. [UPB. 108]

DONNELLAN, Lieutenant Colonel MACLAUGHLIN, in Caltrons, County Galway, a Roman Catholic licensed to bear a sword, a case of pistols, and a gun, 30 March 1705. [HMC.Ormond.ii.475]

THE PEOPLE OF IRELAND, 1600-1699, PART FOUR

DORMER, MATTHEW, born 1620, an apprentice merchant, a witness before the High Court of the Admiralty of England in April 1642. [TNA.HCA13.58/18]

DORRAGH, JAMES GALLAGHER MACEDMOND, late of Kilmore, County Mayo, was proclaimed a traitor and rebel on 14 December 1674. [HMC.Ormonde.ii.342/3]

DOWDALL, EDWARD, of Athirtee, County Louth, 1611. [Carew mss]

DOWDALL, HENRY, in Athearne, County Meath, a Roman Catholic licensed to bear a sword, 30 March 1705, [HMC.Ormond. ii.75]

DOWDALL, JOSEPH, in Corcullentragh, County West Meath, a Roman Catholic licensed to bear a sword, a case of pistols, and a gun, 30 March 1705. [HMC.Ormond.ii.475]

DOWLE, WILLIAM, a merchant in Dublin City, 1611. [Carew mss]

DOWRICH, THOMAS, born 1596 in Cork, Captain of a Regiment of Foot, a witness before the High Court of the Admiralty of England in March 1646. [TNA.HCA13.60.461]

DOYLE, MICHAEL, born 1649, died 9 May 1703, his wife Ann ...., born 1645, died 9 June 1722. [Baldoyle MI, County Dublin]

DRAPER, RICHARD, master of the Providence of Waterford from Waterford to Port Dublin in 1705. [TNA.SP63.366.63]

DUELL, DANIEL, a sailor from Wexford, aboard the privateer Patrick of Jersey, 1650. [TNA.HCA.13.251]

DUFF, ALEXANDER, Mayor of Waterford 1616, refused to take the Oath of Supremacy. [Carew mss.1617.184]

DUFFE, HUGH MCDERMOD, in County Wicklow, was pardoned in Dublin on 23 July 1608. [HMC.Hastings.iv.32]

DUFFET, GEORGE, an English Protestant, in Galway town, 1657. [HHG.appx.XXXVI]

DUKE, MARY, daughter of Sir Henry Duke late of Lecarrowlonbyogge, County Roscommon, and wife of Sir John Jephson, 7 March 1632. [CPRI]

THE PEOPLE OF IRELAND, 1600-1699, PART FOUR

DULLAINE, MATHEW, transported by Captain Bryan Fitzpatrick for service under the King of Sweden, 1630. [APCE.1630.1304]

DULLANEY, THOMAS, granted a pass to go to Ireland 30 January 1656. [Cal.SPDom.1655.577]

DUNCAN, JOHN, ["Jan Doncken"], an Irish soldier, married Anne Thomson, ["Anneke Taemssen"], from Scotland, widow of William Livingston, ["Willem Lieviston"], in Leiden, Holland, 11 July 1603. [Leiden Marriage Register]

DUNGELSON, THOMAS, merchant aboard the Speedwell of Strangford from Strangford to Irvine, Scotland, 1615. [UPB.102]

DUNGAN, MARIA EUPHEMIA, born in Xeres, Spain, Viscountess Duncan of Clare, Ireland, wife of William, Lord Viscount Dungan of Clare, a grant of naturalization in Ireland, 1654.

DUNGAN, URSULA, born in Xeres, Spain, daughter of William, Lord Viscount Dungan, a grant of naturalization in Ireland, 1654.

DUNGAN, WALTER, born in Xeres, Spain, son and heir apparent of William, Lord Viscount Dungan, a grant of naturalization in Ireland, 1654.

DUNN, DANIEL, in Brittas, Queen's County, a Roman Catholic licensed to bear a sword, 30 March 1705. [HMC.Ormond.ii.475]

DUNSANY, Lord Baron RANDAL, in Dunsany, County Meath, a Roman Catholic licensed to bear a sword, a case of pistols, and a gun, 30 March 1705. [HMC.Ormond.ii.475]

DWYER, Captain THOMAS, in Bellacomnisk, County Tipperary, a Roman Catholic licensed to bear a sword, a case of pistols, and a gun, 30 March 1705. [HMC.Ormond.ii.475]

DYLLON, GEORGE, of Killeigh, Dublin, 1611. [Carew mss]

EDNEY, Captain, and THOMAS EDNEY, with 2000 acres in the precinct of Clogher, County Tyrone, 1611. [Carew mss. 1611.130]

EDWARDS, JAMES, granted a pass to go to Ireland 29 April 1656. [Cal.SPDom.1655.581]

THE PEOPLE OF IRELAND, 1600-1699, PART FOUR

EELES, JOHN, Dean of Waterford, 1705. [TNA.SP44.75.14]

ELLIS, EDMUND, late of Lisburn, County Antrim, a petition, 31 July 1697. [CTP.XLVI.93]

ELLIS, ROBERT, a mercer in London, drew lands in the barony of Deece, County Meath, 1659. [CSPI; 1903.343]

ENASSE, TIRLAGH MCSHANE, in County Wicklow, was pardoned in Dublin on 23 July 1608. [HMC.Hastings.iv.32]

ENGLAND, DAVID, in Enis, County Clare, a Roman Catholic licensed to bear a sword, a case of pistols, and a gun, 30 March 1705. [HMC.Ormond.ii.475]

ENGLAND, STEVEN, settled in Bilbao, Spain, around 1607, petitioned for naturalisation in Castille and Leon around 1621. [AGS.CC.leg.1116]

ENGLISH, JAMES, shoemaker in Cashelton, County Kildare, was pardoned in Dublin on 23 July 1608. [HMC.Hastings.iv.32]

ESMONDE, Sir LAWRENCE, with 2000 acres in Wexford, 1616. [Carew mss.1616.168]

EUSTACE, JAMES, in Yeomanstown, County Kildare, a Roman Catholic licensed to bear a sword, a case of pistols, and a gun, 30 March 1705. [HMC.Ormond.ii.475]

EUSTACE, PATRICK, in County Galway, 'a tory, thief or robber', to be apprehended and tried, 1692. [HMC.Ormonde.ii.449]

EVANS, GEORGE, the elder, in Ballygrenane, County Limerick, will, 1710. [DRD]

EVANS, ..., granted a pass to go to Ireland 16 May 1656. [CalSPDom. 1655.582]

EVERARD, MATTHIAS, in Randalstown, County Meath, a Roman Catholic licensed to bear a sword, a case of pistols, and a gun, 30 March 1705. [HMC.Ormond.ii.475]

EWERS, WILLIAM, born in County Kildare 1660, enlisted as a horseman of the King's Guard in 1674. [HMC.Ormonde.ii.237]

FALK, WILLIAM, in Barony of Loughty, County Cavan, 1630. [BL.Add.MS.4770]

FANE, JOHN, master of the Sunday of Ardglass, at Carrickfergus in 1615. [UPB.94]

FARLO, MARTIN, soldier of the train band of Kinsale under Captain Josias Farlo, besieged by the rebels in 1642. [IC.ii.p604]

FARMER, JOHN, master of the Unity of Youghall, from Youghall to Bilbao, Spain, and return, 1705. [TNA.SP44.390.435]

FARRELL, FERGUS, born in County Longford 1650, brown hair, enlisted as a horseman of the King's Guard in 1675. [HMC.Ormonde.ii.237]

FAY, GEORGE, brother and heir of Jeffry Fay of Tromroe, County West Meath, 18 December 1628. [CPRI]

FELYN, JOHN BOYE, master of the Gift of Strangford, 1614. [UPB.106]

FERMIN, JOHN, born 1604, a notary public from Tralee, County Kerry, a witness before the High Court of the Admiralty of England in October 1645. [TNA.HCA13.60.214/274]

FEWSTER, ELIZABETH, daughter of William Fewster in Richmond, Surrey, who died in June 1646, drew lands in the barony of Upper Iveagh, County Down, 1659. [CSPI; 1903.178/343]

FIELD, WILLIAM, son and heir of James Field late of Dublin City, 17 March 1631. [CPRI]

FINCH, CHRISTOPHER, born 1592, a skipper in Dublin, a witness before the High Court of the Admiralty of England in April 1643. [TNA.HCA13.58/510]

FINDING, ANN, spouse of Christopher Eustace of Cradock's Town, County Kildare, a petition 1697. [CTP.XLIV.35]

FINGLASS, MARY, wife of Edward Dowde, daughter and heiress of Roger Finglass of Porterston, County Dublin, 29 December 1631. [CPRI]

FISH, JOHN, a gentleman with 2000 acres in the precinct of Loughte, County Cavan, 1611. [Carew mss.1611.130]

FISHER, Sir EDWARD, with 1000 acres in Wexford, 1616. [Carew mss. 1616.168]

FISHER, HENRY, in Dublin city, 25 February 1628. [CPRI]

FISHER, JOHN, was granted a pass to go to Ireland 29 April 1656. [Cal.SPDom.1655.581]

FITZGERALD, EDWARD, transported by Captain Bryan Fitzpatrick for service under the King of Sweden, 1630. [APCE.1630.1304]

FITZGERALD, EDWARD, son and heir of William Fitzgerald late of Piercetown, County West Meath, 15 March 1631. [CPRI]

FITZGERALD, GARRET, son and heir of John Oge Fitzgerald late Dermany, County Waterford, 20 September 1631. [CPRI]

FITZGERALD, GERALD, was transported by Captain Bryan Fitzpatrick for service under the King of Sweden, 1630. [APCE.1630.1304]

FITZGERALD, GERALD, grandchild and heir of Garret Fitzgerald late of Ballyfoline, County Limerick, and ward of John Fitzgerald, 18 June 1631. [CPRI]

FITZGERALD, JAMES MORRYS OGE, of Templestown, County Cork, was pardoned in Dublin on 12 December 1607. [HMC.Hastings.iv]

FITZGERALD, JOHN, of the Shyan, County Cork, and his spouse Ellis, a petition, 1626. [APCE.1626.86]

FITZGERALD, JOHN, [1], was transported by Captain Bryan Fitzpatrick for service under the King of Sweden, 1630. [APCE.1630.1304]

FITZGERALD, JOHN, [2], was transported by Captain Bryan Fitzpatrick for service under the King of Sweden, 1630. [APCE.1630.1304]

FITZGERALD, MAURICE, son and heir of John Fitzgerald late of Kilrush, 20 March 1628, [CPRI]; a petition, 1629. [APCE.1629.376]

FITZGERALD, MYLES, was transported by Captain Bryan Fitzpatrick for service under the King of Sweden, 1630. [APCE.1630.1304]

FITZGERALD, RICHARD, was appointed Summonister of the Court of Exchequer on 3 September 1629. [CPRI]

FITZGERALD, THOMAS, [1], was transported by Captain Bryan Fitzpatrick for service under the King of Sweden, 1630. [APCE.1630.1304]

FITZGERALD, THOMAS, [2], was transported by Captain Bryan Fitzpatrick for service under the King of Sweden, 1630. [APCE.1630.1304]

FITZGERALD, WILLIAM and EDMOND, sons and heirs of Thomas Oge Fitzgerald late of Ballyfoline, County Limerick, 18 June 1631. [CPRI]

FITZGERALD, WILLIAM, son and heir of Edmond Fitzgerald late of Boolane, County Limerick, 20 December 1632. [CPRI]

FITZJAMES, DANIEL OGE, son and heir of Daniel Meagh Fitzjames late of Disarte, County Cork, 3 December 1632. [CPRI]

FITZMARCUS, JAMES LYNCH, a Catholic, in Galway town, 1640. [HHG.appx.XXXVI]

FITZPATRICK, BRYAN, a Captain in the service of the King of Sweden, 1630. [APCE.1630.1304]

FITZPATRICK, BRYAN, son and heir of Daniel Fitzpatrick late of Gortnaclea, Queen's County, 11 February 1632. [CPRI]

FITZPATRICK, DERMONT, transported by Captain Bryan Fitzpatrick for service under the King of Sweden, 1630. [APCE.1630.1304]

FITZPATRICK, EDMOND, transported by Captain Bryan Fitzpatrick for service under the King of Sweden, 1630. [APCE.1630.1304]

FITZPATRICK, JOHN MCKEALAGH, was granted 120 acres in the barony of Rosclogher, County Leitrim, 17 January 1632. [CPRI]

FITZPATRICK, Colonel JOHN, petitioned re his estate in Ireland, 1673. [SPDom.1673.212]

FITZRICHARD, WILLIAM, son and heir of Richard Fitzwilliam Gibbon late of Kiltoege, County Cork, 21 May 1631. [CPRI]

FITZROBERT, JOHN BLAKE, a Catholic, in Galway town, 1640. [HHG.appx.XXXVI]

FITZSTEPHEN, STEPHEN, son and heir of David Terry Fitzstephen late Alderman of Cork, 24 MARCH 1631. [CPRI]

FITZSYMON, CHRISTOPHER, a merchant in Dublin, husband of Barbara White, will, 1710. [DRD]

FITZWALTER, NICOLAS, WHITE, mayor of Waterford 1615, refused to take the Oath of Supremacy. [Carew mss.1617.184]

FITZWILLIAM, EDWARD, son and heir of James Galway Fitzwilliam late of Kinsale, County Cork, 13 July 1631. [CPRI]

FITZWILLIAMS, Sir THOMAS, of Meryouge, Dublin, 1611. [Carew mss]

FLETCHER, HENRY, was appointed Captain, Constable and Commander of Ballinefadd Fort, County Sligo, with ten men, 17 June 1628. [CPRI]

FLOWERDEW, THOMAS, with 1000 acres in the precinct of Colinkernan, County Fermanagh, 1611. [Carew mss.1617.130]

FLYNN, JOHN, master and merchant of the <u>Sunday of Ardglass</u>, from Dundrum to Wyre, 1615. [UPB.102]

FOLLIOT, Lord THOMAS, Baron of Ballyshannon, probate, 1697. [PCC]

FONTE, ADAM, born 1574, a merchant from Galway, a witness before the High Court of the Admiralty of England in December 1627. [TNA.HCA13.46/460]

FORREST, JASPER, born 1606 in Cork, a merchant, a witness before the High Court of the Admiralty of England in October 1627. [TNA.HCA13.46.313/366]

FORSTALL, EDMOND, in Garteens, County Kilkenny, a Roman Catholic licensed to bear a sword, a case of pistols, and a gun, 30 March 1705. [HMC.Ormond.ii.475]

FORSTALL, REDMOND, transported by Captain Bryan Fitzpatrick for service under the King of Sweden, 1630. [APCE.1630.1304]

FORSTALL, THOMAS, born 1601, a gentleman from Kilmallock, Limerick, a passenger aboard the <u>Gift of God</u> at Bilbao, Spain, in February 1642, a witness before the High Court of the Admiralty of England in September 1642. [TNA.HCA13.58.239]

THE PEOPLE OF IRELAND, 1600-1699, PART FOUR

FORSTER, CHARLES, son and heir of Richard Forster an alderman of the city of Dublin, 2 February 1629. [CPRI]

FORSTER, Ensign NATHANIEL, at Carrickfergus, letter, 1673. [SPDom. 1673.391]

FORWARD, JOHN, of Castle Forward, County Donegal, husband of Anne, will, 1709. [DRD]

FOUCHIER, JAMES, from France, a grant of denization in Ireland, 16 June 1615. [IPR]

FOWKE, JOHN, in Drogheda, probate 1658 PCC. [TNA]

FOX, BRASIL, was granted the manor of Kilcoursie, in King's County, on 18 August 1628. [CPRI]

FREEMAN, THOMAS, born 1626, a merchant in Dublin, a witness in the High Court of the Admiralty of England in April 1646. [TNA.HCA1.59.701]

FRENCH, ANDREW, master of the George of Aran, captured by Parliamentary forces when bound from Aran Islands to Nantes, France, in 1652. [TNA.HCA.30.627]

FRENCH, ARTHUR, in Clooniquin, County Roscommon, a Roman Catholic licensed to bear a sword, a case of pistols, and a gun, 30 March 1705. [HMC.Ormond.ii.476]

FFRENCH, EDMOND, resident of Galway, 11 April 1652. [HHG, appx.xxxii]

FRENCH, GREGORY, born 1604, from Galway, a witness in the High Court of the Admiralty of England in May 1628. [TNA.HCA13.47.199/203]

FRENCH, JAMES, resident of Galway, 26 October 1652. [HHG, appx.xxxii]

FRENCH, JOHN, master of the Peter of Wexford, captured by Parliamentary forces in 1642. [TNA.HCA.13.58.158]

FRENCH, JOHN, master of the pink Eagle of Limerick, from Limerick to San Sebastian, Spain, and return, 1705. [TNA.SP44.390.401]

FRENCH, JOSEPH, was appointed joint Searcher, Gauger, Packer, and Weigher of the port of Cork on 25 May 1629. [CPRI]

FRENCH, NICHOLAS, son and heir of Walter French of Ballitory, County Wexford, 8 December 1628. [CPRI]

FRENCH, NICHOLAS, master of the St Michael of Galway, from Galway to San Sebastian, Spain, and return, 1705. [TNA.SP44.390.375/457]

FRENCH, Sir OLIVER, resident of Galway, 26 October 1652. [HHG, appx.xxxii]

FRENCH, PATRICK, formerly in Dublin now in Duras, County Galway, a Roman Catholic licensed to bear a sword, a case of pistols, and a gun, 30 March 1705. [HMC.Ormond.ii.476]; died 5 June 1708, will, 1709. [DRD]

FRENCH, RICHARD, was appointed joint Searcher, Gauger, Packer, and Weigher of the port of Cork on 25 May 1629. [CPRI]

FRENCH, THOMAS, died 28 October 1629. [Galway MI][HHG]

FRENCH, THOMAS, master of the Minerva of Dublin, from Dublin to Cadiz or Alicante, Spain, and return, 1705. [TNA.SP44.393.75]

FRENCH, WARDEN, resident of Galway, 26 October 1652. [HHG, appx.xxxii]

FRERE, TOBIAS, gentleman in Harlston, drew lands in the south west quarter of the barony of Lecale, County Down, 1659. [CSPI; 1903.173/342]

FURLONG, Captain JAMES, in Dublin City, a Roman Catholic licensed to bear a sword, a case of pistols, and a gun, 30 March 1705. [HMC.Ormond.ii.476]

FURLONGE, THOMAS, son and heir of Philip Furlonge of Craigmenan, County Wexford, 6 December 1628. [CPRI]

GALLAGHER, JAMES, in County Roscommon, 'a tory, thief or robber', to be apprehended and tried, 1692. [HMC.Ormonde.ii.449]

GALLAGHER, WILLIAM, yeoman, late of Court, County Sligo, was proclaimed a traitor and rebel on 14 December 1674. [HMC.Ormonde.ii.342/3]

GALWAY, EDWARD, born 1595 in Kinsale, a merchant, a witness in the High Court of the Admiralty of England in November 1638. [TNA.HCA13.54.266]

GALWAY, WILLIAM, in Cork City, a Roman Catholic licensed to bear a sword, 30 March 1705. [HMC.Ormond.ii.476]

GAMBOLD, THOMAS, master of the John Baptist of Limerick, captured by Parliamentary forces when bound from Limerick to St Malo, France, in 1647. [TNA.HCA.15.2]

GARDNER, JOHN, in Barony of Loughty, County Cavan, 1630. [BL.Add.MS.4770]

GARDNER, THOMAS, master of the Alice of Londonderry, captured by Parliamentary forces when bound from Londonderry to Chester, England, in 1643. [TNA.HCA.13.61.176]

GARDNER, WILLIAM, in Barony of Loughty, County Cavan, 1630. [BL.Add.MS.4770]

GARRALDINE, GARRETT, born 1581, a merchant from Waterford, a witness in the High Court of the Admiralty of England in July 1622. [TNA.HCA13.43.2.175]

GARRYVOGE, TIEGE, a yeoman in County Cork, 'a tory, thief or robber', to be apprehended and tried, 1692. [HMC.Ormonde.ii.449]

GARTH, JOHN, drew lands in the Barony of Deece, County Meath, 1659. [CSPI; 1903.343]

GARVEN, THOMAS, master of the Jennett of Belfast, captured by Parliamentary forces when bound from Bordeaux, France to Carrickfergus in 1644. [TNA.HCA.13.59.204]

GEE, ROBERT, was presented to the prebend of Tascoffin in the cathedral of Ossory; the vicarages of Burres and Straboe in the Diocese of Leighlin and the vicarage of Ardeaghe in the Diocese of Kildare, 19 December 1628. [CPRI]

THE PEOPLE OF IRELAND, 1600-1699, PART FOUR

GEFFERIES, JOHN, drew lands in the south east quarter of the Barony of Lecale, County Down, 1659. [CSPI; 1903.342]

GENINS, THOMAS, settled in Kinsale at Christmas 1641. [IC.ii.p.604]

GEOGHEGAN, Colonel BRYAN, in Donore, West Meath, a Roman Catholic licensed to bear a sword, a case of pistols, and a gun, 30 March 1705. [HMC.Ormond.ii.476]

GEOGHEGAN, DARLY, a shoemaker of Kenlandstown, County Wicklow, took the Oath of Allegiance and Supremacy to King Charles II, on 27 October 1668.

GEOGHEGAN, HUGH, in Castletown, County West Meath, a Roman Catholic licensed to bear a sword, a case of pistols, and a gun, 30 March 1705. [HMC.Ormond.ii.476]

GEOGHEGAN, Major WILLIAM, in Dublin City, a Roman Catholic licensed to bear a sword, 30 March 1705. [HMC.Ormond.ii.476]

GERALD, Sir JOHN FITZEDWARD, in County Cork, 1 March 1632. [CPRI]

GERNON, ANTHONY, of Agher Pallice, County Meath, 1611. [Carew mss]

GERNON, WILLIAM, born in County Meath 1643, black hair, enlisted as a horseman of the King's Guard in 1673. [HMC.Ormonde.ii.237]

GERRALD, THOMAS, of Ilanfdhobogh, a juror at Blackfriars, County Waterford, 5 September 1617. [Carew mss.1617.184]

GERRARD, PETER, master of the brigantine Eagle of Dublin, from Ireland to Bilbao and return, 1705. [TNA.SP44.392.72]

GETHING, RICHARD, born 1608, an armiger from Cork, a witness before the High Court of the Admiralty of England in December 1647. [TNA.HCA13.62.65]

GILBERT, CLAUDIUS, in Limerick, a grant of naturalization, 1656.

GILBERT, GEORGE, born 1611, a merchant in Dublin, a witness before the High Court of the Admiralty of England in October 1644. [TNA.HCA13.59.518]

GILBERT, JOHN, master of Katherine of Waterford, captured by Parliamentary forces when bound from La Rochelle, France, to Bantry in 1651. [TNA.HCA.13.251.i]

GILL, ROBERT, a butcher in Dublin, took the Oath of Allegiance and Supremacy to King Charles II, on 1 July 1667.

GLASSE, TEIGE FITZJOHN, son and heir of John Fitzteige O'Swyllyvane late of Kilkrendry, County Cork, 8 March 1632. [CPRI]

GOGANE, WILLIAM, son and heir of William Gogane later of Bearnehealy, County Cork, 19 May 1632. [CPRI]

GONZALES, EMMANUEL, master of the St Clara of Waterford, 1648. [TNA.HCA.23.15.239]

GOOKIN, THOMAS, a merchant in Kinsale, owner of the Hopewell, from there to Maryland after 1664, seized there by the Deputy Governor. [ActsPCCol.1668.765]

GORE, Captain ARTHUR, a member of the House of Commons in Ireland, formerly an officer in the Earl of Donegal's Regiment, 1705. [TNA.SO1.15.338]

GORE, JOHN, born in County Down 1645, enlisted as a horseman of the King's Guard in 1673. [HMC.Ormonde.ii.237]

GORE, RALPH, was granted the lands of Dromnenagh, County Donegal, 9 January 1630. [CPRI]

GORMANSTOWN, Lord Viscount ANTHONY, in Gormanstown, County Dublin, a Roman Catholic licensed to bear a sword, a case of pistols, and a gun, 30 March 1705. [HMC.Ormond.ii.476]

GOSSE, MARTIN, born 1603 in Youghal, a seaman aboard the Alice, a witness before the High Court of the Admiralty of England in November 1644. [TNA.HCA13.59.543

GOSTE, ROBERT, master of the Moses of Carrickfergus, 1615. [UPB.98]

GOUGH, JAMES, of Waterford, his sister Barbara, and her son Patrick, an agreement, 1 June 1605. [CPRI]

THE PEOPLE OF IRELAND, 1600-1699, PART FOUR

GOUTHWER, THOMAS, in Barony of Loughty, County Cavan, 1630. [BL.Add.MS.4770]

GOVEN, THOMAS, a tailor in Dublin, took the Oath of Allegiance and Supremacy to King Charles II, on 6 July 1669.

GOYNE, ALEXANDER, merchant in Portaferry, aboard the George of the Isle of Man, from Dundrum and Portaferry to Workington, England, in 1615. [UPB.103]

GRACE, ALEXANDER, of Castlannegard, County Limerick, was pardoned in Dublin on 12 December 1607. [HMS.Hastings.iv]

GRACE, EDMOND, transported by Captain Bryan Fitzpatrick for service under the King of Sweden, 1630. [APCE.1630.1304]

GRACE, OLIVER, a gentleman in Shanganagh, Queen's County, will, 1708. [DRD]

GRACE, PEIRCE, transported by Captain Bryan Fitzpatrick for service under the King of Sweden, 1630. [APCE.1630.1304]

GRADIE, DONOGH, son and heir of James Gradie late of Fossagmore, County Clare, 15 March 1632. [CPRI]

GRADY, JAMES, born 1599 in Waterford, a ship's carpenter aboard the Samuel, a witness before the High Court of the Admiralty of England in April 1623. [TNA.HCA13.44.111]

GRANTEBERRAE, ..., a merchant in Waterford, 1678. [LRS.36.15]

GRATRAX, WILLIAM, of Newaughmroe, a juror at Blackfriars, County Waterford, 5 September 1617. [Carew mss.1617.184]

GRAY, THOMAS, examination, 6 January 1654. [TCD.ms819.206]

GREAME, FERGUS, with 300 acres in Wexford, 1616. [Carew mss. 1616.168]

GREEN, HENRY, in Dublin, a letter, 1705. [NAS.CH12.12.365]

GREENHILL, WILLIAM, minister of Stepney, drew lands in the barony of Upper Iveagh, County Down, 1659. [CSPI; 1903.43/343]

THE PEOPLE OF IRELAND, 1600-1699, PART FOUR

GRIELL, JOHN, a grant of naturalization in Ireland, 1655, also an Act in 1662. [Patent Roll, 14-15 Car ii].

GROFTEN, ALBERT, born in Osanau near Amsterdam, Holland, a merchant in Ireland, a grant of naturalisation in Ireland, 1655.

GROSS, MARTIN, master of the Hare of Dublin, was captured by Parliamentary forces when bound from Dublin to Beaumaris, Wales, in 1642. [TNA.HCA.13.62]

GROVE, WILLIAM, in Barony of Loughty, County Cavan, 1630. [BL.Add.MS.4770]

GRUNCE, JAMES, from Waxford, Munster, seaman aboard the ship Elloner of London bound for Old Calabar in Guinea, died at sea, probate 1658 PCC. [TNA]

HADSOR, REGINALD, of Dromcath, County Louth, was bonded to build a village at Greaghenefarne, County Leitrim, 27 June 1632. [CPRI]

HANDSOR, RICHARD, of Keppock, County Louth, 2 January 1632. [CPRI]

HAILETT, WILLIAM, born in Rouen, Normandy, France, a grant of naturalization in Ireland, 1655, also in 1662. [Patent Roll, 13-15 Car ii]

HALGAN, DANIEL, born in Dublin, a glazier, took the Oath of Allegiance and Supremacy to King Charles II, on 18 October 1671.

HALL, EDWARD, master aboard the John of Carrickfergus, from La Rochelle, to Carrickfergus, 1615. [UPB]

HALLORAN, JOHN, master of the Success of Dublin, a galley, from Youghal to Cadiz, Spain, and return, 1705. [TNA.SP44.392.74]

HALLORANE, SIMON, master of the Hope of Limerick, from Limerick to Bilbao, Spain, and return in 1706. [TNA.SP44/393/6]

HALS, JEREMY, born 1565, a gentleman in Kinsale, a witness before the High Court of the Admiralty of England in October 1640. [TNA.HCA13.56.272]

HAM, MAURICE, a cooper from Kinsale, died in the West Indies aboard the flyboat Mary in government service, probate 1657 PCC. [TNA]

THE PEOPLE OF IRELAND, 1600-1699, PART FOUR

HAMILTON, JAMES, in Court Hills, County Meath, will, 1710. [DRD]

HAMLET, JOHN, master of the Bride of Londonderry, 1614, [UPB.10]

HAMOND, EDWARD, in Dublin City, a Roman Catholic licensed to bear a sword, a case of pistols, and a gun, 30 March 1705. [HMC.Ormond.ii. 476]

HAMOND, ROBERT, merchant in London, drew lands in the north east and the south east quarters of the barony of Lecale, County Down, 1659. [CSPI; 1903.342]

HAMOND, WILLIAM, deposition, May 1643. [TCD.ms830. 134]

HANNEY, DANIEL, born 1587, a seaman aboard the Trinity of Waterford, a witness before the High Court of the Admiralty of England in November 1628. [TNA.HCA13.47.406]

HANSARD, MARY, a widow in the suburbs of Dublin, will, 1709. [DRD]

HANYLING, DANIEL, formerly a tenant of Lord Courcie, 'driven by poverty to live beyond the seas', petitioned to return to Ireland, 7 July 1615. Carew mss.1615.157]

HARMAN, HUNGERFORD, born in County Catherlough 1643, brown hair, enlisted as a horseman of the King's Guard in 1668. [HMC.Ormonde.ii. 237]

HARMANS, JOHN, an Irish soldier and vagrant, banished from Leiden, Holland, 11 January 1641. [PL. 111]

HARRIN, CONNOR, in County Galway, 'a tory, thief or robber', to be apprehended and tried, 1692. [HMC.Ormonde.ii.449]

HARRIS, JOHN, born 1603, a merchant in Dublin, a witness before the High Court of the Admiralty of England in February 1636. [TNA.HCA13.52.278]

HARRIS, ROBERT, born 1606, a gentleman in Cork aboard the Elizabeth of Youghal, a witness before the High Court of the Admiralty of England in September 1627. [TNA.HCA13.46.310]

HARRIS, WALTER, in Dublin, 1689. [NAS.GD26.8.15]

HARRISON, EDWARD, of the Church of Ireland, a gentleman and a burgess of Belfast from 1680 to 1700. [BMF]

HARRISON, Captain EDWARD, in Magheralave, Lisburn, died 12 October 1700, probate 24 October 1700. [PRONI.T559/23/55]

HARRISON, MICHAEL, of the Church of Ireland, a gentleman and a burgess of Belfast from 1705 to 1709. [BMF]

HART, BRYAN, born in Roscommon 1653, black hair, enlisted as a horseman of the King's Guard in 1672. [HMC.Ormonde.ii.237]

HART, HENRY, was appointed Escheator General for the counties of Tipperary, the Cross, Kerry, and Limerick on 6 May 1628. [CPRI]

HARTPOLL, ROBERT, son and heir of George Hartpoll late of Monkgrange, Queen's County, 5 March 1632. [CPRI]

HARVEY, WALTER, and his wife, granted a pass to go to Ireland 9 April 1656. [Cal.SPDom.1655.580]

HASSAN, RICHARD, born 1606, from Wexford, a seaman on the St George, a witness before the High Court of the Admiralty of England in July 1634. [TNA.HCA13.51.18]

HATFIELD, OGLE, granted a pass to go to Ireland 12 February 1656. [Cal.SPDom.1655.578]

HATTON, EDWARD, was granted land in the Barony of Clankelly, County Fermanagh, to be called the manor of Knockballymore, 13 August 1629. [CPRI]

HAUGHTON, ARTHUR, born 1616, a gentleman in Youghal, a witness before the High Court of the Admiralty of England in February 1647. [TNA.HCA13.60.698]

HAWKERIDGE, JOHN, born 1613, a merchant in Dublin, a witness before the High Court of the Admiralty of England in August 1640. [TNA.HCA13.55.544]

HAWKINS, ROGER, inn-keeper in Mountmellick, Queen's County, husband of Hannah, will, 1709. [DRD]

HAWKINS, WILLIAM, drew lands in the barony of Upper Iveagh, County Down, 1659. [CSPI; 1903.342]

HAWKRID, JOHN, born 1613, a merchant in Dublin, a witness before the High Court of the Admiralty of England in June 1637. [TNA.HCA13.53.189]

HAYES, JOHN, born 1615, a merchant in Dublin, a witness before the High Court of the Admiralty of England in July 1643. [TNA.HCA13.58.588]

HAYES, WALTER, master of the Patrick of Waterford, captured by Parliamentary forces when bound from Dunkirk, France to Dublin in 1642. [TNA.HCA.13.58.18]

HEATH, WALTER, born 1600, from Dublin, passenger in a flyboat, a witness before the High Court of the Admiralty of England in April 1643. [CPRI]

HECKERIFF, WILLIAM, in Barony of Loughty, County Cavan, 1630. [BL.Add.MS.4770]

HECKLEFIELD, GEORGE, in Barony of Loughty, County Cavan, 1630. [BL.Add.MS.4770]

HECKLEFIELD, HENRY, in Barony of Loughty, County Cavan, 1630. [BL.Add.MS.4770]

HELMES, ROBERT, a merchant in Dublin, 1679. [LRS.36.107]

HENDLEY, HENRY, of Ballyhendrine, County Cork, 1 December 1628. [CPRI]

HENDRA, JOHN, master of the Adventure of Dublin, 1643. [TNA.Adm.18.2.14]

HERBERT, Sir EDWARD, an army pensioner in Ireland, a petitioner 1626. [APCE.1626.94]

HERON, JOHN, a gentleman, with 2000 acres in the precinct of Oneylan, County Armagh, 1611. [Carew mss.1611.130]

HEWETSON, Reverend CHRISTOPHER, Chancellor of Christ's, Presbyter of St Patricks, Vicar and Archbishop of Dublin, died 1634. [Swords MI]

THE PEOPLE OF IRELAND, 1600-1699, PART FOUR

HIBBETS, DANIEL, armed with a sword and pike, in Barony of Loughty, County Cavan, 1630. [BL.Add.MS.4770]

HIBBETS, JOHN, armed with a sword and snaphance, in Barony of Loughty, County Cavan, 1630. [BL.Add.MS.4770]

HIBBETS, MOSES, armed with a sword and snaphance, in Barony of Loughty, County Cavan, 1630. [BL.Add.MS.4770]

HIBBETTS, THOMAS, with 1000 acres in Wexford, 1616. [Carew mss. 1616.168]

HILL, JOHN, born 1577, from Kinsale, master of the Gift of God of Cork, captured by Parliamentary forces when bound from St Martins, France, to Cork in 1649, a witness before the High Court of the Admiralty of England in March 1649. [TNA.HCA.13.61.352]

HILLS, JOHN, from Ballehacke, Wexford, died aboard HMC Cornwall, probate 1696. [PCC]

HILL, Sir MOYSES, of Srahanmiller, County Antrim, purchased lands in County Down and Drogheda, 8 February 1631. [CPRI]

HILL, THOMAS, armed with a sword and snaphance, in Barony of Loughty, County Cavan, 1630. [BL.Add.MS.4770]

HILL, SAMUEL, of Affain, a juror at Blackfriars, County Waterford, 5 September 1617. [Carew mss.1617.184]

HILL, WILLIAM, in Barony of Loughty, County Cavan, 1630. [BL.Add.MS. 4770]

HIND, GEORGE, son and heir of William Hinde late of Cnockan Icnogher, County Roscommon, 14 March 1632. [CPRI]

HINES, JARVIS, an English Protestant, in Galway town, 1657. [HHG.appx.XXXVI]

HOARE, THOMAS, master of the Patrick of Waterford, a witness before the High Court of the Admiralty of England in May 1628. [TNA.HCA13.47.164]

HODGES, THOMAS, merchant in London, drew lands in the Barony of Deece, County Meath, 1659. [CSPI; 1903.343]

HOEY, PARSONS, born in County Kildare, brown hair, enlisted as a horseman of the King's Guard in 1676. [HMC.Ormonde.ii.237]

HOLT, NICHOLAS, master of the privateer St Francis of Wexford, 1648-1650. [HMC.Ormonde.i.121][BLO.Carte ms24.602; Carte.ms29.110]

HOOKE, THOMAS, alderman of Dublin, 1656. [IC.ii.837]

HORE, Colonel JOHN, in Shandon, County Waterford, a Roman Catholic licensed to bear a sword, a case of pistols, and a gun, 30 March 1705. [HMC.Ormond.ii.476]

HORE, THOMAS, master of the Patrick of Waterford, witness, June 1628. [TNA.HCA.47.164]

HORNE, WILLIAM, master of the privateer Mary Consolation of Waterford, 1647. [TNA.HCA.13.62; 23.30]

HORROE, JASPER, sergeant of the outlawry in Waterford, 1617. [Carew mss.1617.178]

HORSEMAN, INGRAM, merchant aboard the Moses of Carrickfergus, 1615. [UPB.98]

HOVILLE, WILLIAM, master of the privateer Angel Keeper of Waterford, 1648. [TNA.HCA.15.2]

HOW, JOHN, at the White Hart, Wellbrook, County Tyrone, a letter, 1689. [NAS.GD26.8.16]

HOWELL, THOMAS, a joiner in Dublin, will, 1709. [DRD]

HOWER, JOHN, master of the Hope of Dungarven, captured by Parliamentary forces when bound from Dungarven to St Malo, France, in 1645. [TNA.HCA.15.5]

HOWRENE, JOHN, of County Kerry, was proclaimed a traitor and rebel on 14 December 1674. [HMC.Ormonde.ii.342/3]

HUDSON, GEORGE, drew lands in the south east quarter of the Barony of Lecale, County Down, 1659. [CSPI; 1903.342]

HUETSON, GEORGE, a Lieutenant in Lord Conway's regiment, from Bristol, England, aboard the Jonathan of Minehead bound for Waterford in May 1629. [APCS.1629.471]

HUGHSON, WILLIAM, master of the Julian of Strangford, 1614. [UPB. 106]

HULL, RANDOLL, a merchant in Cork, 1680, letter. [LRS.36.163]

HUMPHREYS, JOHN, armed with a pike, in Barony of Loughty, County Cavan, 1630. [BL.Add.MS.4770]

HUMPHREYS, NATHANIEL, drew lands in the south east quarter of the Barony of Lecale, County Down, 1659. [CSPI; 1903.342]

HUNNINGES, HENRY, a gentleman with 1000 acres in the precinct of Colinkernan, County Fermanagh, 1611. [Carew mss.1617.130]

HUSSEY, Colonel EDWARD, in Westtown, County Dublin, a Roman Catholic licensed to bear a sword, a case of pistols, and a gun, 30 March 1705. [HMC.Ormond.ii.476]

IRISH, TIERLO MAHOHIER, a soldier in Spanish service in Flanders and by 1602 in Spain. [AGS.E.leg 2764]

ISBRAVUL, GERARD, Captain of the Mary Magdalene of Wexford, 1643. [BLO.Carte ms7.267]

ITCHINGHAM, JOHN, of Dunbrody, County Wexford, 1611. [Carew mss]

IVIE, JOSEPH, in Waterford, a will, 1710. [DRD]

JAMES, GERRALD, of Calishell, a juror at Blackfriars, County Waterford, 5 September 1617. [Carew mss.1617.184]

JAQUESS, WILLIAM, in Rossmecarty, parish of Killnerath, Barony of Owny and Arra, County Tipperary, husband of Katherine, will, 1709. [DRD]

JASPERS, JOHN, from Netherlands, a grant of denization in Ireland, 27 February 1635. [IPR]

JEFFERYES, JOHN, constable of Dublin Castle, 1673. [SPDom. 1673.527]

THE PEOPLE OF IRELAND, 1600-1699, PART FOUR

JEFFRAY, JOHN, was presented to the rectories of Rinroane, Ballynydea alias Rathdrowton, and Kilgobban, and the vicarage of Carygiline, in the diocese of Cork, 20 March 1629. [CPRI]

JOHNSON, BARTHOLEMEW, merchant in Carrickfergus, 1615. [UPB.97]

JOHNSON, CORNELIUS, from the Netherlands, a grant of denization in Ireland, 1 December 1619. [IPR]

JOHNSON, HENDRICK, master of the Katherine of Wexford, captured by Parliamentary forces when bound from Wexford to Nantes and St Malo, France, 1646. [TNA.HCA15.2]

JOHNSON, HENRY, master of the Peter of Donaghadee, [?], 1615. [UPB.110]

JOHNSON, HENRY, born 1601, from Dublin, a witness before the High Court of the Admiralty of England, in June 1642. [TNA.HCA13.58.159]

JONES, LEWES, Dean of Cashel was appointed Bishop of Killallowe, 12 February 1632. [CPRI]

JONES, Sir ROGER, with 1000 acres in Wexford, 1616. [Carew mss. 1616.168]

JOYES, JOHN, resident of Galway, 11 April 1652. [HHG, appx.xxxii]

JOYCE, RICHARD, resident of Galway, 26 October 1652. [HHG, appx.xxxii]

JUXON, ARTHUR, drew lands in the Barony of Deece, County Meath, 1659. [CSPI; 1903.343]

JUXON, JOHN, drew lands in the Barony of Deece, County Meath, 1659. [CSPI; 1903.343]

KANAUGH, EDMOND, transported by Captain Bryan Fitzpatrick for service under the King of Sweden, 1630. [APCE.1630.1304]

KARNEY, JAMES, mariner aboard the Lyon, died in Ireland, probate 1657 PCC. [TNA]

KAVANAGH, BRIAN, gentleman in Newtown, County Roscommon, was pardoned in Dublin on 23 July 1608. [HMC.Hastings.iv.32]

KAVENAGH, MORGAN, in Burress, County Catherlogh, a Roman Catholic licensed to bear a sword, a case of pistols, and a gun, 30 March 1705. [HMC.Ormond.ii.476]

KEAGHER, CORNELIUS, master of the Thomas of Galway from Limerick to San Sebastian or Bilbao, Spain, and return, 1705. [TNA.SP44.392.64]

KEAHIZ, CORNELIUS, master of the John of Galway, from Ireland to San Sebastian, Spain, and return, 1705. [TNA.SP44.392.76]

KEARNAN, WILLIAM, from Ballinteber, died in Amsterdam, Holland, probate 1657 PCC. [TNA]

KEARNS, PHILIPE, an Irish priest in Toulouse, France, in 1620. [AMT.CC2620-2625]

KEATING, ARTHUR, son and heir of Oliver Keating late of Kilconway, County Wexford, 15 March 1632. [CPRI]

KEATING, EDMOND, son and heir of Richard Keating late of Cloughardin, County Tipperary, 16 March 1631. [CPRI]

KEATING, RICHARD, born 1623, from Ballanycrag in Ireland, a soldier in Flanders, a witness before the High Court of the Admiralty of England, in January 1648. [TNA.HCA13.62.64]

KEATING, RICHARD, master of the privateer Delight of Waterford, 1649. [TNA.HCA.13.250.i]

KELLUM, WILLIAM, in Barony of Loughty, County Cavan, 1630. [BL.Add.MS.4770]

KELLY, DONELL, in Waterford, was pardoned in Dublin on 23 July 1608. [HMC.Hastings.iv.32]

KELLY, EDWARD, born 1616, from Kinsale, coxswain aboard HMS Constant, a witness before the High Court of the Admiralty of England, in February 1642. [TNA.HCA13.59.620]

KELLY, JOHN, in 'Westhefurde in Irland', 1598. His ship damaged, its cargo looted, and two of his men murdered by 'Rid Rannald' in Arran. [RPCS.V.487]

KELLY, UNY ny, daughter and heiress of Roger Owen O'Kelly late of Killen, County Galway, 20 December 1631. [CPRI]

KENNEDY, ALEXANDER, born in Belfast, County Antrim, took the Oath of Allegiance and Supremacy to King Charles II, on 7 November 1672.

KENNEDY, Captain JOHN, in Polenorman, County Tipperary, a Roman Catholic licensed to bear a sword, a case of pistols, and a gun, 30 March 1705. [HMC.Ormond.ii.476]

KENNEDY, RICHARD, a yeoman in County Cork, 'a tory, thief or robber', to be apprehended and tried, 1692. [HMC.Ormonde.ii.449]

KENNY, HENRY, in Dublin, was granted the wardship of William O'Dorran, son and heir of Caher O'Doran, late of Chapel in County Wexford, 18 July 1628. [CPRI]

KENNYE, NICHOLAS, with 500 acres in Wexford, 1616. [Carew mss. 1616.168]

KERNY, PAUL, of Casshall, County Cork, was pardoned in Dublin on 12 December 1607. [HMC.Hastings.iv]

KERSEY, JOHN, born 1603, a merchant in Dublin, a witness before the High Court of the Admiralty of England, in January 1639. [TNA.HCA13.54.396]

KIDDERMINSTER, EDMOND, drew lands in the south east quarter of the barony of Lecale, County Down, 1659. [CSPI; 1903.342]

KIERNAN, JAMES, a gentleman in Dublin, husband of Elizabeth, will, 1709. [DRD]

KINDELAN, EDWARD, granted a pass to go to Ireland 16 May 1656. [CalSPDom.1655.582]

KINGELY, DARBY, master of the Neptune of Limerick, from Youghal to Bilbao, Spain, 1705. [TNA.SP44.390.400]

KINGSLAND, Lord Viscount NICHOLAS, in Kingsland, County Dublin, a Roman Catholic licensed to bear a sword, a case of pistols, and a gun, 30 March 1705. [HMC.Ormond.ii.476]

KINGSMILL, Sir JOHN, was granted 1766 acres in the precinct of Lifer, Barony of Raphoe, County Donegal, to be called the manor of Castlefyn, 28 May 1631. [CPRI]

KINNINGTON, BENJAMIN, in Barony of Loughty, County Cavan, 1630. [BL.Add.MS.4770]

KIRWAN, MARCUS, resident of Galway, 11 April 1652. [HHG, appx.xxxii]

KIRWAN, OLIVER, born 1606, a merchant in Galway, a witness before the High Court of the Admiralty of England, in May 1635. [TNA.HCA13.51.530]

KIRWAN, PATRICK, resident of Galway, 26 October 1652. [HHG, appx.xxxii]

KNIVETON, HENRY, born 1596, a gentleman in Cork, a witness before the High Court of the Admiralty of England, in October 1647. [TNA.HCA13.62.11]

KNOCK, JOHN, born 1594, from Culmore, Londonderry, a mariner aboard the Mayflower, a witness before the High Court of the Admiralty of England, in April 1622. [TNA.HCA13.43/2.127]

KNOX, SYMON, master of the Thomas and Ralph of Dublin, captured by Parliamentary forces when bound from Dublin to Liverpool, England, in 1644. [TNA.HCA.13.59.518]

KYRLE, ROBERT, born in Limerick, brown hair, enlisted as a horseman of the King's Guard in 1675. [HMC.Ormonde.ii.237]

LAMPORT, PHILIP, son and heir of James Lamport late of Ballyeire, County Wexford, 29 February 1631. [CPRI]

LANCKEFORDER, HERCULES, merchant and Mayor of Carrickfergus, 1615. [UPB.95]

LANDER, MORRICE, porter of the gates of Waterford, 1617. [Carew mss.1617.178]

LANE, CHARLOTTE, born 'in parts beyond the sea', daughter of Sir George Lane, a grant of naturalization in Ireland, 1654. [IPR]

LANE, WILLIAM, was appointed rector of Nohoval and Knockan cum Dunlo in the Diocese of Ardfert, 4 December 1631. [CPRI]

LANE, WILLIAM, in Lewes, Sussex, drew lands in the Barony of Deece, County Meath, 1659. [CSPI; 1903.343]

LANGFORD, Sir HERCULES, Presbyterian, a gentleman and a burgess of Belfast from 1669 to 1680. [BMF]

LANGHARNE, JOHN, with 1000 acres in Wexford, 1616. [Carew mss. 1616.168]

LANGLEY, THOMAS, of Moyallo, gentleman in County Cork, was pardoned in Dublin on 12 December 1607. [HMC.Hastings.iv]

LEA, JAMES, merchant, churchwarden of Christchurch, Waterford, 1617. [Carew.1617.178]

LEA, JAMES, Controller of the King's Revenues for Waterford, 1617. [Carew mss.1617.178]

LEADBETTER, EDMUND, an army pensioner in Ireland, a petitioner 1626. [APCE.1626.1]

LEADER, RICHARD, born 1608, a merchant or factor in Limerick around 1641, resident in Boston, New England, a witness before the High Court of the Admiralty of England, in August 1650. [TNA.HCA13.58.188]

LEATHES, ALEXANDER, a freeman of Carrickfergus, 1669. [PRONI.Dobbs pp, D163/1]

LEATHES, JOHN, senior, of the Church of Ireland, a merchant and a burgess of Belfast from 1634 to 1667. [BMF]

LEATHES, JOHN, junior, of the Church of Ireland, a merchant and a burgess of Belfast from 1646 to 1693. [BMF]

LEATHES, ROBERT, of the Church of Ireland, a burgess of Belfast from 1669 to 1717. [BMF]

LEATHES, ROBERT, of Liverpool, England, later in Belfast, bound to Barbados, probate 1724. [PRONI.T559/26/109]

LEATHES, WILLIAM, of the Church of Ireland, a merchant and a burgess of Belfast from 1642 to 1660. [BMF]

LEATHES, WILLIAM, a merchant in Belfast, probate 1723. [PRONI.Mussenden pp.D354/55]

LEE, EDWARD, granted a pass to go to Ireland 12 February 1656. [Cal.SPDom.1655.578]

LEE, ROBERT, in Wexford City, a Roman Catholic licensed to bear a sword, 30 March 1705. [HMC.Ormond.ii.476]

LEE, THOMAS, a cook in Dublin city, took the Oath of Allegiance and Supremacy to King Charles II, on 17 January 1666.

LEEDS, MICHAEL, a merchant in Dublin, will, 1708. [DRD]

LEIGH, FRANCIS, in Rathangan, County Kildare, a Roman Catholic licensed to bear a sword, 30 March 1705. [HMC.Ormond.ii.476]

LEIGH, ROBERT, in London, County Catherlogh, a Roman Catholic licensed to bear a sword, 30 March 1705. [HMC.Ormond.ii.476]

LEICESTER, THOMAS, was granted 671 acres in the territory of Fercall in King's County, 20 February 1631. [CPRI]

LEONARTSON, GEORGE, born 1577, a resident of Youghal, a mariner aboard the Elephant a 40 ton Flemish built ship, a witness before the High Court of the Admiralty of England, in January 1623. [TNA.HCA13.44.69]

LEVINGSTON, SAMUEL, granted a pass to go to Ireland 16 May 1656. [CalSPDom.1655.582]

LEVINTHORPE, MARIAN, born 1611, wife of Edward Levinthorpe in Dublin, a witness before the High Court of the Admiralty of England, in July 1642. [TNA.HCA13.58.166]

LEY, PATRICK, merchant, churchwarden of Ladychurch, Waterford, 1617. [Carew.1617.178]

LEYTHES, PETER, born 1633, from Belfast, a sailor aboard the Success from London via the Canaries to New England in 1657. [TNA.HCA.Vol.13/74.pp141-142;Exams.Jan.1662]

LILLYES, JANE, born 1607, wife of Robert Lillyes in Limerick, a witness before the High Court of the Admiralty of England, in October 1645. [TNA.HCA13.60.238]

LINCOLN, GEORGE, searcher of Waterford, 1617. [Carew mss. 1617.178]

LINCOLN, PATRICK, keeper of the 'corn and kett' in Waterford, 1617. [Carew mss.1617.178]

LINCOLN, WILLIAM, 'sworn measurer' of Waterford, 1617. [Carew mss. 1617.178]

LINCOLN, WILLIAM, Controller of the King's Revenues for Waterford, 1617. [Carew mss.1617.178]

LLOYD, PATRICK, born 1627, residing in Strangford, County Down, a seaman aboard the Fortune, a witness before the High Court of the Admiralty of England, in October 1645. [TNA.HCA13.60.280]

LLOYD, PATRICK, born 1625, from Dublin, a seaman aboard the Michael of Wyne, a witness before the High Court of the Admiralty of England, in April 1646. [TNA.HCA13.60.525.159]

LOBE, JOHN, master of the Patrick of Galway, captured by Parliamentary forces when bound from Bilbao, Spain, to Galway in 1648. [TNA.HCA.13.250.ii]

LOCH, JAMES, a yeoman in County Cork, 'a tory, thief or robber', to be apprehended and tried, 1692. [HMC.Ormonde.ii.449]

LOE, Colonel HERCULES, licensed to raise 2100 Irish foot soldiers and transport them to Spain, 19 October 1653. [IC.ii.427]

LOFTUS, Sir ADAM, with 1000 acres in Wexford, 1616. [Carew mss. 1616.168]

LOFTUS, Dr DUDLEY, in Dublin, 1673. [SPDom.1673.527]

LOFTUS, Sir ROBERT, was licenced to hold markets in Mountmellick, Queen's County, 20 July 1631. [CPRI]

LOKINGTON, JOHN, in Barony of Loughty, County Cavan, 1630. [BL.Add.MS.4770]

LONG, DARBY, in Buress, County Catherlogh, a Roman Catholic licensed to bear a sword, a case of pistols, and a gun, 30 March 1705. [HMC.Ormond.ii.476]

LOVELOCK, THOMAS, was granted 4390 acres in the Barony of Rosclogher, County Leitrim, 17 January 1632. [CPRI]

LOW, WILLIAM, in Ballygrenon, Limerick, probate, 1698. [PCC]

LOWTHER, JOHN, in Dublin, probate 1697. [PCC]

LUMBARD, FRANCIS, 'sworn measurer' of Waterford, 1617. [Carew mss.1617.178]

LUSHER, Sir NICHOLAS, a gentleman with 2000 acres in the precinct of Loughte, County Cavan, 1611. [Carew mss.1611.130]

LUSHER, WILLIAM, a gentleman with 1500 acres in the precinct of Loughte, County Cavan, 1611. [Carew mss.1611.130]

LUTTRELL, Colonel HENRY, in Luttrellstown, County Dublin, a Roman Catholic licensed to bear a sword, a case of pistols, and a gun, 30 March 1705. [HMC.Ormond.ii.476]

LYLLES, JAMES, born 1588, an alderman of Limerick, a witness before the High Court of the Admiralty of England, in April 1643. [TNA.HCA13.58.20]

LYNCHE, ALEXANDER, Sheriff of Galway, 26 October 1652. [HHG, appx.xxxii]

LYNCH, ANDREW, born 1624, a merchant in Galway, a witness before the High Court of the Admiralty of England, in November 1644. [TNA.HCA13.59.565]

LYNCHE, JAMES, resident of Galway, 26 October 1652. [HHG, appx.xxxii]

LYNCHE, JEFFREY, resident of Galway, 26 October 1652. [HHG, appx.xxxii]

LYNCHE, JOHN, resident of Galway, 26 October 1652. [HHG, appx.xxxii]

LYNCHE, JOHN, cleric, resident of Galway, 26 October 1652. [HHG, appx.xxxii]

LYNCHE, MARCUS, Mayor of Galway, 26 October 1652. [HHG, appx.xxxii]

LYNCHE, MARTIN, resident of Galway, 26 October 1652. [HHG, appx.xxxii]

LYNCHE, PETER, resident of Galway, 26 October 1652. [HHG, appx.xxxii]

LYNCHE, PIERCE, resident of Galway, 26 October 1652. [HHG, appx.xxxii]

LYNCHE, RICHARD, resident of Galway, 26 October 1652. [HHG, appx.xxxii]

LYNCH, ROBUCK, born 1586, a merchant in Galway, a witness before the High Court of the Admiralty of England, in July 1627. [TNA.HCA13.46.282]

LYNCH, STEPHEN, examination, 17 January 1653. [TCD.ms830. 209]

LYNCH, THOMAS, born 1599, a merchant in Galway, a witness before the High Court of the Admiralty of England, in July 1627. [TNA.HCA13.46.282]

LYNCH, THOMAS, a Roman Catholic merchant in Galway, imprisoned in Proudford's Castle and later Dublin, to be released on condition that he returned to Galway and then move to Connaught, 6 February 1657. [IC.ii.918]

LYNCH, THOMAS, a merchant in Galway, letter, 1678. [LRS.26.22]

LYNCH, WILLIAM, born 1615, a merchant in Galway, a witness before the High Court of the Admiralty of England, in March 1640. [TNA.HCA13.55.429]

LYNDSEY, JAMES, born in Londonderry, a merchant, took the Oath of Allegiance and Supremacy to King Charles II, on 13 April 1670.

LYNE, THOMAS, of Clonkeily, born 1637, died 22 September 1747. [Kilgullane MI]

LYRIE, CORMACK, son and heir of Donell McCartie Lyrie late of Manshie, County Cork, 8 December 1631. [CPRI]

MCANISKE, ROWLAND, master of the Speedwell of Ardglass, 1614. [UPB.106]

MCBRAN, DONELL, brother and heir of James McBran, late of Marshaltown, County Wexford, 24 March 1628. [CPRI]

MACBREHOUNE, HUGH BANE, yeoman, late of Carra, County Sligo, was proclaimed a traitor and rebel on 14 December 1674. [HMC.Ormonde.ii.342/3]

MACBREHOUNE, TIRLAGH, yeoman, late of Carra, County Sligo, was proclaimed a traitor and rebel on 14 December 1674. [HMC.Ormonde.ii.342/3]
Oriel, 1611. [Carew mss]

MCCAFFERY, EDWARD, a mariner from Ireland, died aboard the Sarah at Guinea, probate 1700. [PCC]

MCCANN, PHELIM, a native who was granted land in the Precinct of Oriel, 1611. [Carew mss]

MCCANN, RORY MCPATRICK, a native who was granted land in the Precinct of Oriel, 1611. [Carew mss]

MACCARTHY, CHARLES, Lady Cahir's son in Reghil, County Tipperary, now of Carrighnavar, County Cork, a Roman Catholic licensed to bear a sword, 30 March 1705. [HMC.Ormond.ii.475]

MCCARTHY, DANIEL, superior of the Toulouse seminary, 1661. [ADHG.IG427]

MCCARTIE, DANIEL OGE, of Dungoile, conveyed various lands to Daniel McCartie, grandson and heir of the late Earl of Clancarty, 28 April 1628. [CPRI]

MCCARTY, DONOGH, nephew and heir of Dermot McCarty late of Rochetown, County Cork, 8 February 1632. [CPRI]

MCCARTIE, OWEN, son and heir of Cnoger Oge McCartie late of Carrowcalder, County Cork, 29 November 1632. [CPRI]

MCCOMOGHE, CONVEY, of Loninehan, gentleman, was pardoned in Dublin on 12 December 1607. [HMC.Hastings.iv]

MCCONALIGH, DONNELL, formerly a tenant of Lord Courcie, 'driven by poverty to live beyond the seas', petitioned to return to Ireland, 7 July 1615. [Carew mss.1615.157]

MCCONWAY, TOOLE, to leave Ireland by 28 July 1631 to serve in the Swedish war. 14 July 1631. [CPRI]

MACCREERY, PATRICK, master of the Sunday of Kilclief, 1615. [UPB. 110]

MCCULLIC, PAT, born 1692, died 1750. [Ballyshannon Abbey MI]

MCDAN, CARBRY, a native who was granted land in the Precinct of Oriel, 1611. [Carew Mss]

MCDAN, DONELL, a native who was granted land in the Precinct of Oriel, 1611. [Carew Mss]

MCDONELL, ALEXANDER OGE, a native who was granted land in the Precinct of Oriel, 1611. [Carew Mss]

MCDONELL, CALNAGH, a native who was granted land in the Precinct of Oriel, 1611. [Carew Mss]

MCDONELL, COLLO MCART, a native who was granted land in the Precinct of Oriel, 1611. [Carew Mss]

MCDONELL, COLLO MCEUER, a native who was granted land in the Precinct of Oriel, 1611. [Carew Mss]

MCDONNELL, DERMOT, son and heir of Donell McDonogh Cartie of Dromgarruffe, County Cork, 10 June 1631. [CPRI]

MACDONNEL, DONNEL OGE O'DONNEL, yeoman late in Sligo, County Sligo, was proclaimed a traitor and rebel on 14 December 1674. [HMC.Ormonde.ii.342/3]

MCDONELL, EDMOND GROOME, a native who was granted land in the Precinct of Oriel, 1611. [Carew Mss]

MCDONELL, MULMORY, a native who was granted land in the Precinct of Oriel, 1611. [Carew Mss]

MACDONNOGH, BRYAN, yeoman, late of Coppany, County Sligo, was proclaimed a traitor and rebel on 14 December 1674. [HMC.Ormonde.ii.342/3]

MACDONOUGH, Lieutenant Colonel TERENCE, in Ballygarry, County Mayo, a Roman Catholic licensed to bear a sword, a case of pistols, and a gun, 30 March 1705. [HMC.Ormond.ii.476]

MCENOWE, GERRET, was granted 500 acres in the Barony of Dromahere, County Leitrim, on 11 March 1629. [CPRI]

MCFINAN, CNOGHER, son and heir of Finan McCnogher McDavid O'Mahowne, late of Leamcon, County Cork, 24 March 1631. [CPRI]

MCGEAN, MARGARET, and her son-in-law Thomas O'Fogue, in County West Meath, petitioners, 1626. [APCE.1626.299]

MACGEE, JOHN, master of the <u>Andrew of Ballyshannon</u>, from Ballyshannon to San Sebastian, Spain, and return, 1705. [TNA.SP44.393.83]

MCGEOGHEGAN, THOMAS, son and heir of Arthur McGeoghegan late of Comenstown, County West Meath, 17 November 1631. [CPRI]

MCGERALD, JAMES BIRNE, son and heir of Gerald McLysaghe late of Roscrea, County Tipperary, 18 June 1631. [CPRI]

MCGERROTT, DONOGH MCMORISHE, in County Wexford, was pardoned in Dublin on 23 July 1608. [HMC.Hastings.iv.32]

MCGILLEDUFF, HUGH, a native who was granted land in the Precinct of Oriel, 1611. [Carew Mss]

MCGLANCHY, RORY, born in County Leitrim, was granted 133 acres in the barony of Dromahere, County Leitrim, 29 July 1628. [CPRI]

MCGRANELL, CONNOR MCMURROGH, was granted 667 acres in the Barony and County of Leitrim on 18 May 1629. [CPRI]

MCGRANELL, FERDOROGH MCMELAGHLIN MODERO, was granted 504 acres in the Barony and County of Leitrim on 18 May 1629. [CPRI]

MCGRANELL, GARRETT MCTIRLAGH, was granted 198 acres in the Barony of Mohill, County of Leitrim on 18 May 1629. [CPRI]

MCGRANELL, GEOFFRY BOY, born in County Leitrim, was granted 130 acres in the Barony of Dromahere, County Leitrim, 29 July 1628. [CPRI]

MCGRANELL, GEOFFRY MCROWRY, was granted 356 acres in the Barony and County of Leitrim on 18 May 1629. [CPRI]

MCGRANELL, HUBERT BOY, was granted 85 acres in the Barony of Mohill, County of Leitrim on 18 May 1629. [CPRI]

MCGRANELL, ROSSE, born in County Leitrim, was granted 134 acres in the Barony of Leitrim, 29 July 1628. [CPRI]

MCGRANELL, SHANE BALLAGH, born in County Leitrim, was granted 130 acres in the Barony of Dromahere, County Leitrim, 29 July 1628. [CPRI]

MCGRANELL, TEIGE, born in County Leitrim, was granted 729 acres in the Barony of Dromahere, County Leitrim, 29 July 1628. [CPRI]

MCGRANELL, THADY MCBRIAN, was granted 85 acres in the Barony of Mohill, County Leitrim on 18 May 1629. [CPRI]

MCGRANELL, THADY MCOWEN, was granted 837 acres in the Barony and County of Leitrim on 18 May 1629. [CPRI]

MCGRANELL, TIRLAGH, was granted 510 acres in the Barony and County of Leitrim on 18 May 1629. [CPRI]

MAGRATH, JOHN, of Allevollan, County Tipperary, was created a baronet on 5 June 1629. [CPRI]

MCHUGH, EDMUND MCEVER, was granted 205 acres and Lough Clonclawy, and a salmon fishery in County Leitrim on 18 May 1629. [CPRI]

MCILLICHEAR, JOHN, in Ballechregan, Strabane, 21 April 1664. [NAS.GD112.1.598]

MACKEIENKYN, JOHN, master of the Marigold of Strangford, 1614. [UPB.106]

MACKENISTE, or MACKENEISKEY, EDMUND, master of the Katherine of Ardglass, from Ardglass to Ayr, Scotland, and of the Grace of Strangford, 1615. [UPB.102/106]

MCLAGHLIN, THOMAS CRONE, born in County Leitrim, was granted 1136 acres in the Barony of Dromahere, County Leitrim, 29 July 1628. [CPRI]

MCMURCHIE, DONOGH, a native who was granted land in the Precinct of Oriel, 1611. [Carew Mss]

MCMURREY, DERMOT, born in County Leitrim, was granted 200 acres in the Barony of Dromahere, County Leitrim, 29 July 1628. [CPRI]

MCNEMARRA, DONNEL OGE, of Ferton, County Clare, 1611. [Carew mss]

MCNEMARA, JOHN, son and heir of Maccon McNemara late of Aghnis, County Clare, 25 February 1628. [CPRI]

MCPHELIM, BRIAN MCDONELL, a native who was granted land in the Precinct of Oriel, 1611. [Carew Mss]

MCQUIN, PHELIM, born in County Leitrim, was granted 130 acres in the Barony of Leitrim, 29 July 1628. [CPRI]

MCQUIRK, OWEN, son and heir of Cnogher McOwen McQuirke late of Ballymcquirke, County Cork, 11 July 1631. [CPRI]

MCRAE, JAMES, master of the Bonadventure of Dublin, from Dublin to Cadiz, Spain, 1705. [TNA.SP44/390/320-1]

MCSHANE, DONELL, of Killasebryghe, County Waterford, was pardoned in Dublin on 12 December 1607. [HMC.Hastings.iv]

MCSHANE, DONELL, of Ballingarrea, County Limerick, was pardoned in Dublin on 12 December 1607. [HMC.Hastings.iv]

MCSHANE, DONELL, in Limerick, was pardoned in Dublin on 23 July 1608. [HMC.Hastings.iv.32]

MACSHANE, HUGH, yeoman in County Armagh, was proclaimed a traitor and rebel on 14 December 1674. [HMC.Ormonde.ii.342/3]

MCTIERNAN, CONKEOGH, was granted 295 acres in the Barony of Carrigallen, on 11 March 1629. [CPRI]

MCTIERNAN, TEIG MCMOYLESSA, was granted 160 acres in the Barony of Carrigallen, on 11 March 1629. [CPRI]

MCTIERNAN, TEIGE REOGH, was granted 227 acres in the Barony of Carrigallen, on 11 March 1629. [CPRI]

MCWILLIAM, HUGH MCFARDORROGH, son and heir of Fardorrogh McWilliam of Killavoggy, County Galway, 20 July 1632. [CPRI]

MADDIN, DERMOT, in County Galway, 'a tory, thief or robber', to be apprehended and tried, 1692. [HMC.Ormonde.ii.449]

MAGAN, THOMAS, in Togherstown, County West Meath, husband of Sarah, will, 1710. [DRD]

MAGAWLY. Lieutenant Colonel PATRICK, in Tully, County West Meath, a Roman Catholic licensed to bear a sword, a case of pistols, and a gun, 30 March 1705. [HMC.Ormond.ii.476]

MAGEE, BARTHOLEMEW, in County Galway, 'a tory, thief or robber', to be apprehended and tried, 1692. [HMC.Ormonde.ii.449]

MAGEE, PATRICK, master of the Jonas of Ardglass, 1614. [UPB.106]

MAGHERIE, WILLIAM, of Cloghrisie, County Cork, 19 November 1632. [CPRI]

MAGRAGH, JOHN, in County Roscommon, 'a tory, thief or robber', to be apprehended and tried, 1692. [HMC.Ormonde.ii.449]

MAGUIRE, CORMACK ROE, a rebel in County Fermanagh, 1641. [PRONI.MIC.8.2]

MAGUIRE, EDMUND CARRAGH, a rebel in County Fermanagh, 1641. [PRONI.MIC.8.2]

MAGUIRE, PATRICK MAGILL DUFF, a rebel in County Fermanagh, 1641. [PRONI.MIC.8.2]

MAGUIRE, ROSS GILPATRICK, a rebel in County Fermanagh, 1641. [PRONI.MIC.8.2]

MAGUIRE, TURLAGH MCHUGH MCART, a rebel in County Fermanagh, 1641. [PRONI.MIC.8.2]

MANDERVILLE, JAMES, probably in Kilkenny, 27 October 1632. [CPRI]

MANSFIELD, RALPH, was granted 1000 acres in Kilnaguerdan, precinct of Liffer, Barony of Raphoe, County Donegal, to be called the manor of Kilnaguerdan on 13 July 1631. [CPRI]

MANSFIELD, Captain, with 1500 acres in the precinct of Liffer, County Donegal, 1611. [Carew mss. 1611.130]

MANWARING, KATHERINE, was granted 115 acres in the Barony of Rosclogher, County Leitrim, 17 January 1632. [CPRI]

MARCUS, JACQUES, a merchant from Amsterdam, Holland, a grant of denization in Ireland, 6 September 1608. [IPR]

MARSHALL, ROBERT, transported by Captain Bryan Fitzpatrick for service under the King of Sweden, 1630. [APCE.1630.1304]

MARSHALL, THOMAS, an English Protestant, in Galway town, 1657. [HHG.appx.XXXVI]

MARTEN, EDMOND, born 1605, a merchant in Galway, a witness before the High Court of the Admiralty of England, in July 1627. [TNA.HCA13.46.282]

MARTIN, Colonel GARRET, in Dublin City, a Roman Catholic licensed to bear a sword, a case of pistols, and a gun, 30 March 1705. [HMC.Ormond.ii.476]

MARTINS, JAMES, and his wife Elinor, from the Netherlands, a grant of denization in Ireland, 25 February 1628. [IPR]

MARTIN, JAMES, resident of Galway, 26 October 1652. [HHG, appx.xxxii]

MARTIN, JOHN, was appointed joint Customs Controller of the port of Drogheda on 2 July 1629. [CPRI]

MARTIN, MARGARET, and GILES, daughters and co-heiresses of Francis Martin a merchant late of Galway, 2 February 1631. [CPRI]

MARTYNE, MATHEW, a Catholic, in Galway town, 1640. [HHG.appx.XXXVI]

MARTINE, W., Sheriff of Galway, 26 October 1652. [HHG, appx.xxxii]

MARWOOD, WILLIAM, with 1000 acres in Wexford, 1616. [Carew mss. 1616.168]

MASON, ROBERT, clerk to the Commissioners at Loughrea, to be dismissed, 7 November 1656. [IC.ii.896]

MASTERS, RICHARD, in Denton, Essex, eldest son of Sir Edward Masters of Canterbury, deceased, drew lands in the Barony of Deece, County Meath, 1659. [CSPI; 1903.73/343]

MATHEWS, ARDEL, born in Dundalk 16 53, brown hair, enlisted as a horseman of the King's Guard in 1676. [HMC.Ormonde.ii.237]

MATHEWS, BRYAN, born in County Louth 1656, black hair, enlisted as a horseman of the King's Guard in 1677. [HMC.Ormonde.ii.237]

MATHEWS, THEOBALD, of Annfield, Tipperary, probate 1700. [PCC]

MAYLER, RICHARD, born 1603, a mariner aboard the <u>Mary of Waterford</u>, a witness before the High Court of the Admiralty of England, in October 1644. [TNA.HCA13.59.546]

MAYNE, JAMES, of Irish Kirk near Ballimore, an examination concerning pirates, 15 December 1620. [Carew mss.1620.219]

MAYNES, CHRISTOPHER, in Barony of Loughty, County Cavan, 1630. [BL.Add.MS.4770]

MAYNES, WILLIAM, in Barony of Loughty, County Cavan, 1630. [BL.Add.MS.4770]

MEADE, PEIRCE, born 1611, a merchant in Cork, a witness before the High Court of the Admiralty of England, in April 1642. [TNA.HCA13.57.454]

MEAGH, DAVID, of Kinsale, County Cork, letter of attorney, 6 June 1631. [CPRI]

MEAGHE, PATRICK, merchant aboard the Katherine of Ardglass from Ardglass to Ayr, Scotland, 1615. [UPB.102]

MEARES, BARNABY, drew lands in the Barony of Deece, County Meath, 1659. [CSPI; 1903.343]

MELAND, DANIEL, a sailor from Wexford, aboard the privateer Patrick of Jersey, 1650. [TNA.HCA.13.251]

MELLEFONT, JAMES, son and heir of William Mellefont late of Watersland, County Cork, 4 June 1632. [CPRI]

MERVIN, Captain JAMES, son of Sir Henry Mervin and Lady Christian, was granted lands in County Tyrone to be called the manors of Stoy, Tuchet, and Arleston, 1 July 1631; 29 August 1631. [CPRI]

MICKLETHWAITE, NATHANIEL, drew lands in the Barony of Deece, County Meath, 1659. [CSPI; 1903.343]

MILLER, RICHARD, master of the Mary of Waterford, captured by Parliamentary forces when bound from Waterford to Le Croisic, France, in 1644. [TNA.HCA.13.59.546]

MILLINGTON, WILLIAM, in Barony of Loughty, County Cavan, 1630. [BL.Add.MS.4770]

MILNER, JACOB, book-seller, Essex Street, Dublin, 1695. [NLI]

MINTER, ROBERT, born 1582, a pilot in Galway, a witness before the High Court of the Admiralty of England, in October 1641. [TNA.HCA13.57.235]

MISSETT, MICHAEL, born in Dowdingstown, County Kildare, a merchant, took wthe Oath of Allegiance and Supremacy to King Charles II, on 20 July 1671.

MODELER, PATRICK, a native who was granted land in the Precinct of Oriel, 1611. [Carew mss]

MOGHAN, alias VAUGHAN, DAVID, son and heir of Morris Moghan alias Vaughan late of Kilbraderan, County Limerick, 21 June 1632. [CPRI]

MOGRIDGE, TRISTRAM, born 1608, a factor in Kilfentenan, County Clare, a witness before the High Court of the Admiralty of England, in June 1635. [TNA.HCA13.52.8]

MOIGNE, ABIGAIL, widow of Roger Moigne, and **JOHN GREENHAM,** were granted land in Lisreagh, County Cavan, to be called the manor of Moignhall, 13 July 1629. [CPRI]

MOLYNEX, DANIEL, from Bruges, Flanders, a grant of denization in Ireland, 16 August 1594. [IPR]

MOLYNEX, SAMUEL, from Bruges, Flanders, a grant of denization in Ireland, 16 August 1594. [IPR]

MONDAY, THOMAS, an army pensioner in Ireland, a petitioner 1626. [APCE.1626.91]

MOORE, MARGARET, a spinster in Dublin, will, 1710. [DRD]

MOORE, ROGER, of Ballyna, County Kildare, a licence to alienate lnds in County Meath, 2 March 1632. [CPRI]

MORAN, EDMOND, in County Leitrim, 'a tory, thief or robber', to be apprehended and tried, 1692. [HMC.Ormonde.ii.449]

MORAN, THOMAS, in County Galway, 'a tory, thief or robber', to be apprehended and tried, 1692. [HMC.Ormonde.ii.449]

MORCARTY, JOHN, master of the <u>Margaret and Agnes</u>, from Ireland to Bilbao or San Sebastian, Spain, and return, 1705. [TNA.SP44.392.67]

MORE, GEORGE, armed with a sword, in Barony of Loughty, County Cavan, 1630. [BL.Add.MS.4770]

MORE, ROSSE, transported by Captain Bryan Fitzpatrick for service under the King of Sweden, 1630. [APCE.1630.1304]

MORGAN, THOMAS, master of the <u>James of Youghal</u>, 100 tons, 40 men, 8 gun ship, 1644-1645. [TNA.HCA.15.5]

MORISH, ANDREW, resident of Galway, 11 April 1652. [HHG, appx.xxxii]

MORLEY, FRANCIS, of Tallowe, a juror at Blackfriars, County Waterford, 5 September 1617. [Carew mss.1617.184]

MORLEY, HERBERT, drew lands in the Barony of Deece, County Meath, 1659. [CSPI; 1903.343]

MORONY, THOMAS, master of the Mary of Limerick, from Limerick to Bilbao, Spain, and return, 1705. [TNA.SP44.390.323]

MORRIS, CHARLES, granted a pass to go to Ireland 12 March 1656. [Cal.SPDom.1655.579]

MORRISON, RICHARD, master of the Northsbore of Londonderry bound for Portugal, arrested and imprisoned in Southampton charged with trading with France in 1705. [TNA.SP42.120.61; SP44.105.120]

MOSYER, JOHN, granted a pass to go to Ireland 29 April 1656. [Cal.SPDom.1655.581]

MOTLEY, WALTER, a merchant in Dublin, 1673. [SPDom.1673.527]

MOULSWORTH, ROBERT, a merchant in Dublin, to transport felons in Newgate gaol, Dublin, to Barbados or other English plantation in America, 18 January 1656. [IC.ii.777]; 'died beyond the seas', probate 1657 PCC. [TNA]

MULLIN, JOHN, master of the Providence of Donaghadee, captured by Parliamentary forces when bound from Dublin to Liverpool, England, in 1645. [TNA.HCA.13.248]

MULVY, JOHN, in County Leitrim, 'a tory, thief or robber', to be apprehended and tried, 1692. [HMC.Ormonde.ii.449]

MURDAGH, ANDREW, born in Killileagh, County Down, a blacksmith, took the Oath of Allegiance and Supremacy to King Charles II, on 23 September 1670.

MURPHY, RICHARD, master of the Dove of Dublin, from Ireland to Catelonia, 1705. [TNA.SP42.119.193]

MURPHEY, JAMES, master of the Dove of Dublin, from Cardigan, Wales, to Port Dublin, 1705, [TNA.SP63.366.63]

MURPHY, PATRICK, son and heir of Gerald Murphy of Knocknecrogh, County Carlow, 13 November 1632. [CPRI]

MURPHEY, WILLIAM, master of the Robert of Wexford at Port Dublin, October 1706. [TNA.SP63.366.63]

MURTH, THOMAS, master of the Robert of Dublin, from Dublin to San Sebastian, Spain, and return, 1705. [TNA.SP44.393.95]

MURTIE, GEORGE, searcher of Waterford, 1617. [Carew mss.1617.178]

MURTIE, JOHN, gauger of Waterford, 1617. [Carew mss.1617.178]

NANGLE, Lieutenant Colonel FRANCIS, in Tallahanade, County West Meath, a Roman Catholic licensed to bear a sword, a case of pistols, and a gun, 30 March 1705. [HMC.Ormond.ii.476]

NANGLE, GARRETT, transported by Captain Bryan Fitzpatrick for service under the King of Sweden, 1630. [APCE.1630.1304]

NANGLE, GARRET, in Moyne, County West Meath, a Roman Catholic licensed to bear a sword, a case of pistols, and a gun, 30 March 1705. [HMC.Ormond.ii.476]

NANGLE, PHILIP, son and heir of Walter Nangle late of Rosetown, County West Meath, 23 September 1631. [CPRI]

NANGELL, WILLIAM, transported by Captain Bryan Fitzpatrick for service under the King of Sweden, 1630. [APCE.1630.1304]

NASH, DAVID, a Roman Catholic prisoner in Dublin, to be released on condition that he moved to Connaught, 6 February 1657. [IC.ii.918]

NAYLOR, GEORGE, in Barony of Loughty, County Cavan, 1630. [BL.Add.MS.4770]

NEEDHAM, JOHN, born 1613, a surgeon in Cork, a witness before the High Court of the Admiralty of England, in July 1644. [TNA.HCA13.59.395]

NETTERVILL, JAMES, in Dublin City, a Roman Catholic licensed to bear a sword, 30 March 1705. [HMC.Ormond.ii.476]

NETTERVILL, LUKE, Lord Nettervill's brother, in Dublin City, a Roman Catholic licensed to bear a sword, a case of pistols, and a gun, 30 March 1705. [HMC.Ormond.ii.476]

NETTERVILL, NICHOLAS, of Dowth, County Meath, 1611. [Carew mss]

NEWBURGH, THOMAS, a gentleman in Ballyhayes, Cavan, died in London, probate 1697. [PCC]

NEWMAN, THOMAS, in Barony of Loughty, County Cavan, 1630. [BL.Add.MS.4770]

NEWPORT, JOHN, in Carrick, County Tipperary, petitioned for the grant of the forfeited estates of James Gilligan, George Hoare, Patrick Lea and others, in November 1697. [CTP.XLIX.4]

NICHOLSON, GILBERT, in Dublin, will, 1709. [DRD]

NIELSON, Captain MARMADUKE, an army pensioner in Ireland, 1626. [APCE.1626.301]

NOLAN, THOMAS, a Catholic, in Galway town, 1640. [HHG.appx.XXXVI]

NOLSOR, DAVID, master of the Thomas of Dublin, from Youghal to Bilbao, Spain, and return in 1705. [TNA.SP44.392.54]

NOONANE, HUGH, of County Kerry, was proclaimed a traitor and rebel on 14 December 1674. [HMC.Ormonde.ii.342/3]

NORRIS, Captain JOHN, to transport vagabonds in the precincts of Limerick and Cork to the Caribee Islands, 19 April 1654; to transport prisoners, including three priests and twenty women to Barbados, 4/8 December 1655; [IC.ii.487; 759;761]

NORTH, WILLIAM, in Barony of Loughty, County Cavan, 1630. [BL.Add.MS.4770]

NORTH, WILLIAM, in Barony of Loughty, County Cavan, 1630. [BL.Add.MS.4770]

NOSEWORTHY, EDWARD, minister of St David's, Exeter, drew lands in the Barony of Deece, County Meath, 1659. [CSPI; 1903.343]

NUGENT, CHRISTOPHER, son and heir of Henry Nugent of Killagh, County West Meath, 28 January 1629. [CPRI]

NUGENT, EDMOND, son and heir of James Nugent late of Killinshonick, County West Meath, a ward of Henry Fyninge, 6 December 1631. [CPRI]

NUGENT, Lieutenant Colonel EDWARD, in Mitchelstown, County West Meath, a Roman Catholic licensed to bear a sword, a case of pistols, and a gun, 30 March 1705. [HMC.Ormond.ii.476]

NUGENT, Major GARRET, in Moyne, West Meath, a Roman Catholic licensed to bear a sword, a case of pistols, and a gun, 30 March 1705. [HMC.Ormond.ii.476]

NUGENT, HENRY, an exile in Spain, made a Count there by Charles II of Spain, Governor of Gibraltar, dead by 1705. [TNA.SP44.241.182-183]

NUGENT, JAMES, of Keilmichle, County Cork, a petition re his younger brother Thomas Nugent, 1629. [ACPE.1629.335]

NUGENT, JAMES, of Aghamartin, County Cork, 19 November 1632. [CPRI]

NUGENT, Colonel JAMES, in Castle Nugent, County Longford, a Roman Catholic licensed to bear a sword, a case of pistols, and a gun, 30 March 1705. [HMC.Ormond.ii.476]

NUGENT, JOHN, in Cloncoskreen, County Waterford, a Roman Catholic licensed to bear a sword, a case of pistols, and a gun, 30 March 1705. [HMC.Ormond.ii.476]

NUGENT, Captain MATTHIAS, in Ballynascurry, County West Meath, a Roman Catholic licensed to bear a sword, a case of pistols, and a gun, 30 March 1705. [HMC.Ormond.ii.476]

NUGENT, MICHAEL, in Dublin City, a Roman Catholic licensed to bear a sword, a case of pistols, and a gun, 30 March 1705. [HMC.Ormond.ii.476]

NUGENT, MICHAEL, master of the William of Drogheda from Ireland to Bilbao, Spain, and return in 1705. [TNA.SP44.392.43]

NUGENT, RICHARD, son and heir of Oliver Nugent late of Farrencullen, County West Meath, 14 September 1631. [CPRI]

NUGENT, Lieutenant Colonel ROBERT, in Carlingstown, County West Meath, a Roman Catholic licensed to bear a sword, a case of pistols, and a gun, 30 March 1705. [HMC.Ormond.ii.476]

NUGENT, THOMAS, a pardon of alienation, 19 December 1632. [CPRI]

NUGENT, THOMAS, alias Lord Riverstown, in Pallas, County Galway, a Roman Catholic licensed to bear a sword, a case of pistols, and a gun, 30 March 1705. [HMC.Ormond.ii.476]

NY DUNGANN, HONOR, was pardoned in Dublin on 23 July 1608. [HMC.Hastings.iv.32]

O'BACHRAHAN, PATRICK, of Philipstown, King's County, was pardoned in Dublin on 12 December 1607. [HMC.Hastings.iv]

O'BEIRNE, NICHOLAS, and his wife Margaret Ny Kulinan, 1629. [HHG] [Galway MI]

O'BYNS, PRUDENCE, and JOHN, were granted 620 acres in the Barony of O'Nealan, County Armagh, to be called the manor of Ballywarren, 13 July 1631. [CPRI]

O'BRIAN, CONNOR, gentleman in County Louth, was pardoned in Dublin on 18 January 1608. [HMC. Hastings.iv.29]

O'BRIEN, DANIEL, son and heir of Cormock O'Brian late of Cornemadra, County Westmeath, 5 December 1631. [CPRI]

O'BRIEN, DONAT, son and heir of Cornelius O'Brien late of Lemenagh, County Clare, 27 January 1629. [CPRI]

O'BRYAN, MORROGH, son and heir of Murtagh O'Bryan late of Tullagh, County Clare, 25 February 1628. [CPRI]

O'BRIEN, TIEG, son and heir of Morrogh O'Brien late of Towghessegreny, County Limerick, 30 May 1629. [CPRI]

O'BURRIN, TEIG OGE, born in County Leitrim, was granted 527 acres in the Barony of Leitrim, County Leitrim, 29 July 1628. [CPRI]

O'BYRNE, DONAGH MCEDMUND, in County Wicklow, was pardoned in Dublin on 23 July 1608. [HMC.Hastings.iv.32]

O'BIRNE, CARBRIE, son and heir of Ferrall O'Birne late of Cloone Ichattan, County Roscommon, ward of William O'Molloy, 1 March 1632. [CPRI]

O'BIRNE, JOHN, son and heir of Patrick McFirr O'Birne late of Moyhill, County Carlow, 16 March 1631. [CPRI]

O'CALLAGHANE, CORNELIUS, son and heir of Teige Mcnogher O'Callaghane late of Bantry, County Cork, 7 February 1631. [CPRI]

O'CLERY, FLAN, died 1665, [Ballyshannon Abbey MI]

O'CONNELL, GILLEDANNY, shoemaker in Knockmak, County Meath, was pardoned in Dublin on 23 July 1608. [HMC.Hastings.iv.32]

O'CROWLY, DONOGH, son and heir of Cnogher O'Crowly late of Granarde, County Cork, 24 March 1631. [CPRI]

O'CULLANE, DERMOT, son and heir of Dermot McDonell O'Cullane of Ballincoursie, County Cork, 13 March 1632. [CPRI]

O'CULLANE, TEIGE, born in County Leitrim, was granted 200 acres in the Barony of Dromahere, County Leitrim, 29 July 1628. [CPRI]

O'CURNEENE, DWALLAGH DUFFE, born in County Leitrim, was granted 265 acres in the Barony of Dromahere, County Leitrim, 29 July 1628. [CPRI]

O'DINGAN, RORIE, was granted 668 acres in Fercall, King's County, 20 February 1631. [CPRI]

O'DOGHERTIE, OWEN, yeoman, late of Coulkearny, County Mayo, was proclaimed a traitor and rebel on 14 December 1674. [HMC.Ormonde.ii.342/3]

O'DOLAN, TIRLAGH, was pardoned in Dublin on 23 July 1608. [HMC.Hastings.iv.32]

O'DONNELL, ANTHONY, born 1681, O.F.M., Bishop of Raphoe from 1750 to 1755, died 26 April 1755. [Ballyshannon Abbey MI]

O'DONELLY, EDMOND OGE, a native who was granted land in the Precinct of Oriel, 1611. [Carew Mss]

O'DONNEL, SHANE KITTAGH, yeoman, late a prisoner in County Mayo, was proclaimed a traitor and rebel on 14 December 1674. [HMC.Ormonde.ii.342/3]

O'DONNELL, WALTER, in County Cork, was pardoned in Dublin on 12 December 1607. [HMC.Hastings.iv]

O'DONELLAN, JOHN, son and heir of Owen O'Donellan late of Kilveyne, County Mayo, 9 May 1631. [CPRI]

O'DONELLY, EDMOND OGE, a native who was granted land in the Precinct of Oriel, 1611. [Carew Mss]

O'DOOGENAN, SHANE BALLAGH, was granted 604 acres in the Barony and county of Leitrim on 18 May 1629. [CPRI]

O'DORRAN, WILLIAM, master of the privateer Mary Virgin of Wexford, 1648-1649. [TNA.HCA.13.250.ii]

O'DOWLIN, OWEN, was granted 117 acres in O'Melaghline country, County West Meath, 20 February 1631. [CPRI]

O'DOYNE, SHANE MCMURTAGH, was granted 313 acres on the territory of Iregan alias O'Doyne country, Queen's County, 20 February 1631. [CPRI]

O'DRISCOLL, DENIS, lord of Castlehaven, settled in Spain by 1603. [AGS.GA.leg.611]

O'DWYER, Colonel EDMUND, licensed to transport 3500 Irish into Flanders for the service of the Prince of Conde, 19 October 1653. [IC.ii.428/434]

O'FARRELL, GARRET, of Killinagh, County West Meath, 1626. [APCE.1626.299]

O'GALLAGHER, DONNOGH BOY, yeoman, late of Coolkearny, County Mayo, was proclaimed a traitor and rebel on 14 December 1674. [HMC.Ormonde.ii.342/3]

O'GRADY, DONNOGH MCSHANE, of Fossaghmore, County Clare, 1611. [Carew mss]

O'HAGGAN, BRIEN OGE, a native who was granted land in the Precinct of Oriel, 1611. [Carew Mss]

O'HAGGAN, DONOGH REOGH, a native who was granted land in the Precinct of Oriel, 1611. [Carew Mss]

O'HAGGAN, LAUGHLIN, a native who was granted land in the Precinct of Oriel, 1611. [Carew Mss]

O'HANLON, ARDELL MORE, a native who was granted land in the Precinct of Oriel, 1611. [Carew Mss]

O'HANLON, LAUGHLIN MACREDMOND, yeoman in Killeany, County Armagh, was proclaimed a traitor and rebel on 14 December 1674, wanted dead or alive, reward £10. [HMC.Ormonde.ii.342/3]

O'HANLEN, PATRICK, a gentleman in Ireland a petitioner, 1626. [APCE. 1626.174]

O'HANLON, PATRICK MCMANUS, a native who was granted land in the Precinct of Oriel, 1611. [Carew Mss]

O'HANLON, REDMOND MCFERDOROGH, a native who was granted land in the Precinct of Oriel, 1611. [Carew Mss]

O'HANLON, REDMOND, yeoman in Tonderegee, County Armagh, was proclaimed a traitor and rebel on 14 December 1674, wanted dead or alive, reward £10. [HMC.Ormonde.ii.342/3]

O'HANLON, RORY MCFERFOROGH, a native who was granted land in the Precinct of Oriel, 1611. [Carew Mss]

O'HANLON, SHANE OGE, a native who was granted land in the Precinct of Oriel, 1611. [Carew Mss]

O'HANLON, THORLAGH MACPATRICK GOAM, of Aghyneneclogmullen, yeoman in County Armagh, was proclaimed a traitor and rebel on 14 December 1674. [HMC.Ormonde.ii.342/3]

O'HANLON, TIRLAGH GROOME, a native who was granted land in the Precinct of Oriel, 1611. [Carew Mss]

O'HANLON, SHANE MCSHANE, a native who was granted land in the Precinct of Oriel, 1611. [Carew Mss]

O'HANLON, SHANE MCOGHY, a native who was granted land in the Precinct of Oriel, 1611. [Carew Mss]

O'HARA, CAHELL, was licenced to hold a market in the town of Cruville, County Antrim, 17 December 1631. [CPRI]

O'HART, DONNOGH FITZJOHN, yeoman, late of Knockadoe, County Sligo, was proclaimed a traitor and rebel on 14 December 1674. [HMC.Ormonde.ii.342/3]

O'HART, HUGH MCBRIAN OGE MCRORY, a tory, surrendered to Robert Park, justice of the peace for County Sligo, 9 February 1657. [IC.ii.919]

O'HART, MULMURRY, a tory, surrendered to Robert Park, justice of the peace for County Sligo, 9 February 1657. [IC.ii.919]

O'HEFFERNAN, MATHEW, son and heir of Agheray O'Heffernan of Ballinglany, County Tipperary, 29 November 1628. [CPRI]

O'HIGGIN, BRIARTAGH alias MURTOGH, and his son **DONOUGH ROE O'HIGGIN,** to be tried in Enniskillen for the murder in County Fermanagh of Thomas Green in 1641, 9 May 1655. [IC.ii.668]

O'HINAN, DAVID, and MARCUS O'HINAN, were granted 121 acres in the territory of Ey O'Carroll in King's County, 20 February 1631. [CPRI]

O'HINAN, JOHN, was granted 80 acres in the territory of Ely O'Carroll in King's County, 20 February 1631. [CPRI]

O'KEAVIN, WILLIAM, yeoman, late of Ballyntrohan, County Sligo, was proclaimed a traitor and rebel on 14 December 1674. [HMC.Ormonde.ii.342/3]

O'KELLY, WILLIAM, son and heir of Melaughlin Moyle O'Kelly late of Cloonefall, County Galway, 2 February 1631. [CPRI]

O'KENNEDY, PHILIP, was pardoned in Dublin on 23 July 1608. [HMC.Hastings.iv.32]

O'KINELAN, EDWARD, son and heir of Beaghan O'Kinelan of Ballinekill, County Meath, 23 March 1628. [CPRI]

O'LWYNE, MORTOGHE, of Kilmaclinea, County Cork, was pardoned in Dublin on 12 December 1607. [HMC.Hastings.iv]

O'MAHONE, DANIEL, an Irish priest in Toulouse, France, in 1618. [AMT.CC2615]

O'MAHONE, DONOGH, son and heir of Fynyn Rose O'Mahone late of Pullrich, County Cork, 20 February 1631. [CPRI]

O'MAHONY, CONOR, born 1594 in County Cork, a Jesuit in Portugal, died 1656.

O'MEAGHER, THOMAS, son and heir of John O'Meagher late of Boolybane, County Tipperary, 3 December 1632. [CPRI]

O'MELLAN, CAHIR, a native who was granted land in the Precinct of Oriel, 1611. [Carew Mss]

O'MOORE, ROGER, son and heir of Callough O'Moore late of Kilmainham Wood, County Meath, 16 August 1628. [CPRI]

O'MOROGHOW, DONOUGH, formerly a tenant of Lord Courcie, 'driven by poverty to live beyond the seas', petitioned to return to Ireland, 7 July 1615. [Carew mss.1615.157]

O'MULLOY, ARTE, transported by Captain Bryan Fitzpatrick for service under the King of Sweden, 1630. [APCE.1630.1304]

O'MULRIAN, SHANE alias JOHN GLASS, son and heir of Donell McShane Glass O'Mulrian of Gortkelly, County Tipperary, 11 Decembrr 1631. [CPRI]

O'MULLVOGHERY, CAHILL, was granted 372 acres in the Barony of Carrigallen, County Leitrim, on 11 March 1629. [CPRI]

O'MULVOGHERY, OWEN, born in County Leitrim, was granted 276 acres in the Barony of Dromahere, County Leitrim, 29 July 1628. [CPRI]

O'MULVY, OWNY MCBRIAN, was granted 94 acres in the Barony and County of Leitrim on 18 May 1629. [CPRI]

O'MURPHY, CORMUCK RAVER, yeoman in County Armagh, was proclaimed a traitor and rebel on 14 December 1674. [HMC.Ormonde.ii.342/3]

O'MURPHY, DANIEL MACMURPHY MACTHORLAGH ROE, yeoman in County Armagh, was proclaimed a traitor and rebel on 14 December 1674. [HMC.Ormonde.ii.342/3]

O'MURPHY, HUGH TURR, of County Armagh, was proclaimed a traitor and rebel on 14 December 1674. [HMC.Ormonde.ii.342/3]

THE PEOPLE OF IRELAND, 1600-1699, PART FOUR

O'MURPHY, JAMES MACNICHOLAS, yeoman in County Armagh, was proclaimed a traitor and rebel on 14 December 1674. [HMC.Ormonde.ii.342/3]

O'MUYNSHAN, OWYN, of Ballaga, County Clare, was pardoned in Dublin on 12 December 1607. [HMC.Hastings.iv]

O'NEALE, ART. MCCARRON, a native who was granted land in the Precinct of Oriel, 1611. [Carew Mss]

O'NEALE, ART TIRLOGH, a native who was granted land in the Precinct of Oriel, 1611. [Carew Mss]

O'NEALE, BRIAN MCMELAGHLIN, a native who was granted land in the Precinct of Oriel, 1611. [Carew mss]

O'NEALE, BRYAN MOYLE, of County Armagh, was proclaimed a traitor and rebel on 14 December 1674. [HMC.Ormonde.ii.342/3]

O'NEALE, DONELL MCHENRY, a native who was granted land in the Precinct of Oriel, 1611. [Carew Mss]

O'NEALE, DONN MCTIRLOGH, a native who was granted land in the Precinct of Oriel, 1611. [Carew Mss]

O'NEALE, HENRY MCSHANE, a native who was granted land in the Precinct of Oriel, 1611. [Carew Mss]

O'NEALE, HUGH MCCARBRY, a native who was granted land in the Precinct of Oriel, 1611. [Carew Mss]

O'NEALE, NEALE MCTIRLOGH, a native who was granted land in the Precinct of Oriel, 1611. [Carew Mss]

O'NEALE, OWEN MCHUGH, a native who was granted land in the Precinct of Oriel, 1611. [Carew mss]

O'NEALE, OWEN VALLY, a native who was granted land in the Precinct of Oriel, 1611. [Carew Mss]

O'NEALE, PHELIM MCTIRLOGH BRASELOGH, a native who was granted land in the Precinct of Oriel, 1611. [Carew Mss]

O'NEALE, SHANE MCTIRLOGH, a native who was granted land in the Precinct of Oriel, 1611. [Carew Mss]

O'NEIL, DANIEL, an Irish soldier, married Cathelijne Waghenere of Memmingen, Pfalz, in Leiden, Holland, 29 December 1606. [PL.202]

O'NEIL, GROGAN, an Irish soldier imprisoned in Canongate Tolbooth, Edinburgh, released to go to Flanders to fight for King William, 1691. [RPCS.XVI.649]

O'QUINE, DANIEL, formerly a tenant of Lord Courcie, 'driven by poverty to live beyond the seas', petitioned to return to Ireland, 7 July 1615. [Carew mss.1615.157]

O'QUINN, Mr JEREMY, a minister in Ulster, to repair to Dublin for instruction before moving to Connaught, 12 June 1655. [IC.ii.682]

O'QUIN, NEERE, a native who was granted land in the Precinct of Oriel, 1611. [Carew Mss]

O'QUIN, PHELIM, a native who was granted land in the Precinct of Oriel, 1611. [Carew Mss]

O'RORKE, BRIAN MCHUGH, born in County Leitrim, was granted 500 acres in the Barony of Dromahere, County Leitrim, 29 July 1628. [CPRI]

O'RORKE, BRIAN MCULICK, was granted 223 acres in the Barony of Carrigallen, County Leitrim, on 11 March 1629. [CPRI]

O'RORKE, CON PHELIM, was granted 180 acres in the Barony of Carrigallen, County Leitrim, on 11 March 1629. [CPRI]

O'RORKE, DONOGH MCSHANE, was granted 493 acres in the Barony of Carrigallen, County Leitrim, on 11 March 1629. [CPRI]

O'RORKE, PHELIM MCBRIAN MCCONNOR, was granted 246 acres in the Barony of Carrigallen, County Leitrim, on 11 March 1629. [CPRI]

O'RORKE, TEIG OGE MCTEIG MCULICK, was granted 389 acres in the Barony of Dromahere, County Leitrim, on 11 March 1629. [CPRI]

O'RORKE, TIRLAGH MCMELAGHLIN MCCONNOR, was granted 295 acres in the Barony of Carrigallen, County Leitrim, on 11 March 1629. [CPRI]

THE PEOPLE OF IRELAND, 1600-1699, PART FOUR

O'SULLIVAN, DERMOT, from 'Aghatubbrid' in Ireland, residing in Spain in 1621, a testimonial. [AGS.CC.leg.116]

OGE, PHELIM MCOWEN, a native who was granted land in the Precinct of Oriel, 1611. [Carew Mss]

OGE, PHILIP, brother and heir of William Fitzhenry Barry Oge, late of Rincorran, County Cork, 23 June 1631. [CPRI]

OLDFERS, WYBRAND, master of the Peter of Londonderry, 1614. [UPB.8]

OLFERTSON, JOHN, from Holland, a grant of denization in Ireland, 15 February 1612. [IPR]

OLFERTSON, WYBRANT, from Holland, a grant of denization in Ireland, 15 February 1612; 6 February 1618. [IPR]

OLIVER, FRANCIS, master of the Patrick of Waterford, 1647. [TNA.HCA.15.2]

ORMSBY, PETER, born in Roscommon, a gentleman, took the Oath of Allegiance and Supremacy to King Charles II, on 23 September 1669.

ORMSBY, RICHARD, a merchant in Ireland, co-owner of the Hopewell of Galway trading with Barbados pre 1668. [ActsPCCol.1668.744]

OSBORNE, Lieutenant EDWARD, at Carrickfergus, letter, 1673. [SPDom.1673.391]

OVERTON, NATHANIEL, in Ireland, 1643, eldest son and heir of Henry Overton late of London. [CSPI.1903.104]

OXBURROUGH, Colonel HENRY, in Bovin, King's County, a Roman Catholic licensed to bear a sword, a case of pistols, and a gun, 30 March 1705. [HMC.Ormond.ii.476]

OXORTH, THOMAS, armed with a sword and pike, in Barony of Loughty, County Cavan, 1630. [BL.Add.MS.4770]

OXORTH, VINCENT, armed with a snaphance, in Barony of Loughty, County Cavan, 1630. [BL.Add.MS.4770]

PAGE, AUSTEN, armed with a halberd, in Barony of Loughty, County Cavan, 1630. [BL.Add.MS.4770]

PALMER, WILLIAM, armed with a snaphánce, in Barony of Loughty, County Cavan, 1630. [BL.Add.MS.4770]

PANCKARD, FREDERICK, a merchant from the Netherlands, a grant of denization in Ireland, 24 March 1638. [IPR]

PANCKART, JAMES, from Duren in the province of Gulick, Germany, a grant of denization in Ireland, 5 March 1646. [IPR, 21 Car 1]

PAR, MYLES, in Barony of Loughty, County Cavan, 1630. [BL.Add.MS.4770]

PAR, MYLES, jr., in Barony of Loughty, County Cavan, 1630. [BL.Add.MS.4770]

PAR, WILLIAM, in Barony of Loughty, County Cavan, 1630. [BL.Add.MS.4770]

PARKS, JOHN, born 1608, a merchant from Carrickfergus, County Antrim, a witness, April 1639. [TNA.HCA.55.5; 55.2]

PARNELL, JOHN, armed with a musket, in Barony of Loughty, County Cavan, 1630. [BL.Add.MS.4770]

PARSONS, RICHARD, son and heir of Sir Laurence Parsons, 29 November 1632. [CPRI]

PARSONS, WILLIAM, with 2000 acres in the precinct of Clogher, County Tyrone, 1611. [Carew mss. 1611.130]; grant of land in the Barony of Clogher, County Tyrone, 29 July 1629.[CPRI]

PARTRIDGE, JOHN, cutler in London, drew lands in the Barony of Deece, County Meath, 1659. [CSPI; 1903.128/343]

PARTRIDGE, WILLIAM, born in Queen's County, flaxen hair, enlisted as a horseman of the King's Guard in 1663. [HMC.Ormonde.ii.237]

PATTISON, EDWARD, drew lands in the Barony of Deece, County Meath, 1659. [CSPI; 1903.343]

PAYNE, VALENTINE, in Strangford, County Down, a witness, April 1629. [TNA.HCA.48.134]

PEALE, RICHARD, in Barony of Loughty, County Cavan, 1630. [BL.Add.MS.4770]

PEARARFIUT, JACOB, master of the Margaret and Elizabeth of Waterford, captured by Parliamentary forces in 1649. [TNA.HCA.3.232]

PENNY, JOHN, master of the Elisabeth of Londonderry, 1615. [UPB.32]

PEPPARD, ANTHONY, of Glascarick, County Wexford, conveyed the priory of Glascaricke to his son Patrick Peppard, 19 January 1592. [CPRI]

PEPPER, PHILIP, in Barony of Loughty, County Cavan, 1630. [BL.Add.MS.4770]

PEPPER, RICHARD, in Barony of Loughty, County Cavan, 1630. [BL.Add.MS.4770]

PERKINS, WILLIAM, armed with a sword and pike, in Barony of Loughty, County Cavan, 1630. [BL.Add.MS.4770]

PERKINSON, THOMAS, armed with a snaphance, in Barony of Loughty, County Cavan, 1630. [BL.Add.MS.4770]

PERRY, JOHN, in Woodruffe, County Tipperary, will, 1710. [DRD]

PERSONNS, WILLIAM, with 1500 acres in Wexford, 1616. [Carew mss. 1616.168]

PETERSON, CHRISTOPHER, from Alkmaar, Holland, a grant of denization in Ireland, 11 December 1655. [Patent Roll, Commonwealth, 1.3/29]

PETERSON, PETER, from Holland, a grant of denization in Ireland, 22 December 1617. [IPR]

PETERSON, PETER, master of the Elizabeth of Wexford, captured by Parliamentary forces when bound from Wexford to Bilbao, Spain, in 1648. [CSPI.1647-1660.5]

PETTIT, GERALD, son and heir of Thomas Pettit late of Irishton, County West Meath, 11 March 1631. [CPRI]

PEYRS, HENRY, with 1000 acres in Wexford, 1616. [Carew mss. 1616.168]

PIERCE, NICHOLAS, granted a pass to go to Ireland 28 February 1656. [Cal.SPDom.1655.579]

PIERS, Lady HONORIA, a widow in Dublin, will, 1710. [DRD]

PIGGOTT, Mrs MARY, with five children in Londonderry, widow of a captain of Dragoons in the garrison of Londonderry during the siege, a petition, 1698. [CTP.LV.85]

PIKE, JOHN, master of the John of Carrickfergus, from La Rochelle, France, to Carrickfergus, 1615. [UPB]

PILL, PETER, yeoman in County Armagh, was proclaimed a traitor and rebel on 14 December 1674. [HMC.Ormonde.ii.342/3]

PINNOCK, MICHAEL, son and heir of Thomas Pinnock late of Dublin City, 1 April 1631. [CPRI]

PLUNKETT, Colonel CHRISTOPHER, in Lagore, County Meath, a Roman Catholic licensed to bear a sword, a case of pistols, and a gun, 30 March 1705. [HMC.Ormond.ii.476]

PLUNKETT, NICHOLAS, in Dunshally, County Dublin, a Roman Catholic licensed to bear a sword, 30 March 1705. [HMC.Ormond.ii.476]

PLUNKETT, PATRICK, a merchant in Drogheda, husband of Margaret Cheevers, will, 1708. [DRD]

PLUNKETT, ROBERT, born 1623, from Cork, a mariner aboard the Sampson, a witness, September 1647. [TNA.HCA.13.62.3]

POOLE, FRANCIS, born 1590, from Youghal, a mariner aboard the Ann and Elisabeth, a witness, June 1644. [TNA.HCA.59.291]

POOLE, RICHARD, born 1618, a mariner aboard the Ann and Elisabeth, a witness, June 1644. [TNA.HCA.59.291]

POORE, EDWARD, born 1605, from Waterford, a seaman aboard the Trinity of Waterford, a witness, November 1628. [TNA.HCA.47.406]

POORE, WALTER, was pardoned in Dublin on 23 July 1608. [HMC.Hastings.iv.32]

POPE, JOHN, born 1598, Customs Officer at Waterford, a witness before the High Court of the Admiralty of England, in May 1642. [TNA.HCA13.58.86]

PORTER, THOMAS, keeper of the 'corn and kett' in Waterford, 1617. [Carew mss.1617.178]

PORTER, THOMAS, in Barony of Loughty, County Cavan, 1630. [BL.Add.MS.4770]

POWER, CORNELIUS, born in Cadphard, County Kildare, a glover, took the Oath of Allegiance and Supremacy to King Charles II, on 14 January 1671.

POWER, EDMOND, of Monetrym, a juror at Blackfriars, County Waterford, 5 September 1617. [Carew mss.1617.184]

POWER, JOHN, transported by Captain Bryan Fitzpatrick for service under the King of Sweden, 1630. [APCE.1630.1304]

POWER, Major JOHN, in Clashmore, County Waterford, a Roman Catholic licensed to bear a sword, a case of pistols, and a gun, 30 March 1705. [HMC.Ormond.ii.476]

POWER, MORRYS, of Adamstown, a juror at Blackfriars, County Waterford, 5 September 1617. [Carew mss.1617.184]

POWER, NICOLAS, of Dunhill, a juror at Blackfriars, County Waterford, 5 September 1617. [Carew mss.1617.184]

POWER, PETER, of Ballygaron, a juror at Blackfriars, County Waterford, 5 September 1617. [Carew mss.1617.184]

POWER, THOMAS, of Dwaygle, a juror at Blackfriars, County Waterford, 5 September 1617. [Carew mss.1617.184]

POWER, WALTER, brother and heir of Thomas Power late of Ballivallickine, County Waterford, 2 June 1632. [CPRI]

PRAT, JOHN, drew lands in the Barony of Deece, County Meath, 1659. [CSPI; v1903.343]

PRENDERGRASS, Captain THOMAS, was granted the lands of Roger O'Shaghnessey in the Barony of Kiltarton, County Galway, 1697. [CTP.XLIII.75]

PRENDERGAST, PIERSE, son and heir of Edmond Duffe Prendergast late of Tullaghemollane, County Tipperary, 24 September 1632. [CPRI]

PRENDERGASTE, ROBERT, brother and heir of James Prendergast late of Newcastle, County Tipperary, 1 December 1628.[CPRI]

PRENDERGAST, WALTER, son and heir of Robert Prendergast late of Polinetarry, County Tipperary, 19 July 1631. [CPRI]

PRESSICK, SAMUEL, born in Athlone, County Roscommon, a glover, took the Oath of Allegiance and Supremacy to King Charles II, on 11 January 1671.

PRESTLY, JOHN, born in Drogheda 1659, brown hair, enlisted as a horseman of the King's Guard in 16... [HMC.Ormonde.ii.237]

PRESTON, ROBERT, born 1600, a gentleman in Rogerstown, near Dublin, a witness before the High Court of the Admiralty of England, in June 1633. [TNA.HCA13.50.333]

PROBY, THOMAS, in Dublin, to build the Queen's dog kennel there, 20 May 1706. [TNA.SO.1.15.323]

PROCTOR, ANTHONY, prebend of Desert and Killmolleran, Diocese of Lismore, also vicar of Kilmaydon, Diocese of Waterford, 16 May 1628. [CPRI]

PROCTOR, JOHN, drew lands in the Barony of Deece, County Meath, 1659. [CSPI.1903.343]

PURCELL, Lieutenant JOHN, in Crumline, County Dublin, a Roman Catholic licensed to bear a sword, a case of pistols, and a gun, 30 March 1705. [HMC.Ormond.ii.476]

THE PEOPLE OF IRELAND, 1600-1699, PART FOUR

PURCELL, Colonel NICHOLAS, in Loghmore, County Tipperary, a Roman Catholic licensed to bear a sword, a case of pistols, and a gun, 30 March 1705. [HMC.Ormond.ii.476]

PURCELL, PHILLIP, of Ballyfoyle, 27 October 1632. [CPRI]

PURCELL, RICHARD, son and heir of Peter Purcell late of Lismaine, County Kilkenny, 17 February 1632. [CPRI]

PURCELL, Colonel TOBY, Governor of Dungannon, purchased lands in County Tipperary around 1700 from John Butler. [TNA.SP44.242.2-5]

PURCELL, WILLIAM, transported by Captain Bryan Fitzpatrick for service under the King of Sweden, 1630. [APCE.1630.1304]

PYKE, JOHN, master of the John of Carrickfergus, trading between La Rochelle, France, and Ulster in 1615. [UPB.98]

QUIN, JAMES, merchant in Galway, and his wife Eleanor Joyes, 1649. [Galway MI][HHG]

QUINN, Father THOMAS, Abbot of Blessed Mary's Abbey of Saimer, died 30 May 1669. [Ballyshannon Abbey MI]

QUINT, WALTER, master of the Swallow of Youghal, captured by Parliamentary forces when bound from Youghal to Bristol, England, in 1644. [TNA.HCA.13.246]

QUISY, WILLIAM, armed with a sword and pike, in Barony of Loughty, County Cavan, 1630. [BL.Add.MS.4770]

RAMELTON, AGNES, in Dublin, Caledon, and Castle Leslie, letters 1690-1730. [NAS.GD45.14.238]

RANAKERS, THOMAS, of West Carborow, Cork, died in Lancashire, probate 1659 PCC. [TNA]

RANSFORD, Sir MARK, an alderman of Dublin, will, 1709. [DRD]

RAY, CHARLES, a merchant in and a member of the Youghal Corporation in S1684. [CA.Youghal Corporation Minute Book]

READER, JAMES, in Barony of Loughty, County Cavan, 1630. [BL.Add.MS.4770]

READER, JOHN, armed with a pike, in Barony of Loughty, County Cavan, 1630. [BL.Add.MS.4770]

READER, ROBERT, in Barony of Loughty, County Cavan, 1630. [BL.Add.MS.4770]

REARDANE or GRIAGH, CNOGHER, of County Kerry, was proclaimed a traitor and rebel on 14 December 1674. [HMC.Ormonde.ii.342/3]

REDLAKE, RICHARD, born 1617, from Lismore, County Waterford, a merchant, a witness, April 1636. [TNA.HCA.52.351/2]

REDMOND, CHARLES, in Dublin City, a Roman Catholic licensed to bear a sword, a case of pistols, and a gun, 30 March 1705. [HMC.Ormond.ii. 476]

REEVES, JAMES, of Stroucally, a juror at Blackfriars, County Waterford, 5 September 1617. [Carew mss.1617.184]

REIGH, LAUGHLIN, a native of Clamore, Galway, a salt boiler, took the Oath of Allegiance and Supremacy to King Charles II, on 29 July 1664.

REILLY, CORNELIUS, born 1609 in Ireland, an inventory, Rotterdam, Holland, 1639. [GAR.ONA.430.66.83]

REILLY, Lieutenant Colonel JOHN, late in Conlin, County Cavan, later of Ballymacadd, County Meath, a Roman Catholic licensed to bear a sword, a case of pistols, and a gun, 30 March 1705. [HMC.Ormond.ii. 476]

REILLY, Captain OWEN, born 1676, died 18 May 1728. [Drung MI]

REMINGTON, Sir ROBERT, with 2000 acres in the precinct of Liffer, County Donegal, 1611. [Carew mss. 1611.130]

REYNELLS, EDWARD, of the Church of Ireland, a gentleman and a burgess of Belfast from 1660 to 1682. [BMF]

REYNOLDS, HUMFRY, was granted 332 acres in the Barony of Mohill also 1147 acres in the Barony of Leitrim, on 18 May 1629. [CPRI]

REYNOLDS, KEADAGH, in County Leitrim, 'a tory, thief or robber', to be apprehended and tried, 1692. [HMC.Ormonde.ii.449]

REYNOLDS, ROBERT, land grant of 1000 acres in County Louth, 1656. [IC.ii.775]

RIANE, Captain DANIEL, a soldier, from St Malo, France, aboard the Unity of Cork, bound for Ireland, intercepted by the Parliamentary navy in 1642. [TNA.HCA.13.58.1]

RICE, Lieutenant Colonel JOHN, in Hospital, County Limerick, a Roman Catholic licensed to bear a sword, a case of pistols, and a gun, 30 March 1705. [HMC.Ormond.ii.477]

RICE, THOMAS, of Dingleicuish, County Kerry, 1 March 1632. [CPRI]

RICHARDS, JENKIN, master of the brigantine Swallow of Waterford from Dublin to San Lucar in Spain, 1705. [TNA.SP44.390.349]

RICKMAN, JAMES, born in the Netherlands, a perfumer in the parish of St Keven, Dublin City, a grant of denization in Ireland, 12 July 1641. [Patent Roll, 17 Car 1.part 2]

RIDGBY, JOHN, of the Church of Ireland, a tanner and a burgess of Belfast from 1655 to 1669. [BMF]

RIDGEWAY, GEORGE, a gentleman, with 2000 acres in the precinct of Clogher, County Tyrone, 1611. [Carew mss. 1611.130]

RIDGEWAY, Sir THOMAS, with 2000 acres in the precinct of Clogher, County Tyrone, 1611. [Carew mss. 1611.130]

RIELY, DANIEL, born in County Down, a butcher, took the Oath of Allegiance and Supremacy to King Charles II, on 3 December 1667.

ROBINSON, GEORGE, of Dublin City, deceased by 1611. [Carew mss]

ROBINSON, JOHN, armed with a sword and pike, in Barony of Loughty, County Cavan, 1630. [BL.Add.MS.4770]

ROBINSON, JONATHAN, master of the Mary of Youghall, from Youghall to Bilbao, Spain, 1705. [TNA.SP44.351]

ROBINSON, LAWRENCE, Chancellor of St Patrick's Cathedral in Armagh, 20 May 1628. [CPRI]

ROBISON, HENRY, master of the Henry of Londonderry, 1614. [UPB.28]

ROCH, CLEMENT, master of the 170 ton privateer <u>Clement of Wexford</u>, 1643. [BL.Carte ms7.267]

ROCH, DAVID, born 1585, burgomaster of Limerick, a witness before the High Court of the Admiralty of England in April 1643. [TNA.HCA13.58.20]

ROCH, DOMINICK, a Roman Catholic resident of Kinsale, 1641. [IC.ii.p605]

ROCHE, JOHN, born 1602, a merchant from Cork, a witness before the High Court of the Admiralty of England in October 1627. [TNA.HCA.46.313/386]

ROCHE, JOHN, son and heir of Thomas Roche of Limerick, 25 February 1628. [CPRI]

ROCHE, JORDAN, late alderman of Limerick, deceased, father of Christian, Anstance, Katherine and John, petition, 1656. [IC.ii.784]

ROCH, MARK, master of the <u>Eagle of Limerick</u> captured by Parliamentary forces when bound from Limerick to La Rochelle, France, in 1649. [TNA.HCA.13.250.i]

ROCH, MORRIS, in Cork City, a Roman Catholic licensed to bear a sword, a case of pistols, and a gun, 30 March 1705. [HMC.Ormond.ii.476]

ROCHE, PAUL, master of the <u>Hare of Wexford</u>, 1643. [TNA.HCA30.849.552]

ROCH, ROBERT, born in Waterford, a shoemaker, took the Oath of Allegiance and Supremacy to King Charles II, on 21 May 1667.

ROCH, THEOBALD, son and heir of David Roch of Leicklash, County Cork, 1 December 1628. [CPRI]

ROCH, THOMAS, with 2000 acres in the precinct of Clogher, County Tyrone, 1611. [Carew mss. 1611.130]

ROCHE, WILLIAM, born 1588, a seaman from Wexford aboard the <u>St George of Galway</u>, a witness before the High Court of the Admiralty of England in November 1634. [TNA.HCA13.51.18]

ROCHFORT, NICHOLAS, master of the 50 ton privateer Mary Magdalene of Wexford, 1649. [TNA.HCA.30.855.278]

ROE, JAMES, of Ballinteggart, yeoman in County Armagh, was proclaimed a traitor and rebel on 14 December 1674. [HMC.Ormonde.ii.342/3]

ROGERS, GEORGE, in Ashgrove, County Cork, husband of Mary, will, 1710. [DRD]

ROGERS, RICHARD, of the Ross, County Kerry, 1611. [Carew mss]

ROHD, NICHOLAS, in the parish of St Mary's, Dublin, husband of Rachel Rohd, will, 1708. [DRD]

RONAN, WILLIAM, sergeant of the outlawry in Waterford, 1617. [Carew mss.1617.178]

RONEY, PETER, master of the William of Ardglass, 1614. [UPB.106]

ROSE, LEVANDER, from Graunte, the Netherlands, a grant of denization in Ireland, 29 January 1620. [IPR]

ROSSITER, JOHN, master of the privateer Mary and John of Wexford, 1646-1649. [TCD.ms819, fo.203][TNA.HCA.13.250]

ROTH, RICHARD, in the city of Kilkenny, 27 October 1632. [CPRI]

ROTHERAM, THOMAS, was granted 1704 acres in the Barony of Rosclogher, County Leitrim, 17 January 1632. [CPRI]

ROURKE, MARY NY DONELL, alias, was granted 5011 acres of land in the Barony of Dromahere, County Leitrim, to be called the manor of Preston, 22 December 1631. [CPRI]

ROUSE, JOHN, a yeoman in County Cork, 'a tory, thief or robber', to be apprehended and tried, 1692. [HMC.Ormonde.ii.449]

ROW, HENRY, born in Dublin, a shoemaker, took the Oath of Allegiance and Supremacy to King Charles II, on 11 January 1666.

ROWE, JAMES, transported by Captain Bryan Fitzpatrick for service under the King of Sweden, 1630. [APCE.1630.1304]

ROWKINS, JOHN, in Barony of Loughty, County Cavan, 1630. [BL.Add.MS.4770]

ROWLEY, JOHN, merchant in Coleraine, 1615. [UPB.87]

RUBBENS, JACOB, from the Netherlands, a grant of denization in Ireland, 6 February 1638. [IPR]

RUDDOCK, JOSEPH, master of the Hannah of Cork, a brig, from Jamaica to Bristol, England, in 1705. [TNA.SP63.365.127]

RUMNEY, SYMON, clerk in Otford, Kent, was assigned land in the Barony of Iffa and Offa, County Tipperary, by William Viner goldsmith of London, 1654. [CSPI.1903.305]

RUSSELL, EDWARD, with 1500 acres in the precinct of Liffer, County Donegal, 1611. [Carew mss. 1611.130]

RUSSELL, JOHN, drew lands in the Barony of Deece, County Meath, 1659. [CSPI; 1903.343]

RUSSELL, RICHARD, of the manor of Dryneham, County Dublin, 31 December 1628. [CPRI]

RUTLEDGE, RICHARD, was licenced to hold markets in the town of Strade, County Mayo, 20 February 1631. [CPRI]

RYAN, DANIEL, born 1620, from Sallacot in Ireland, fought for the King of France against Spain, a witness, April 1642. [TNA.HCA.58.1]

RYAN, DERMOT, a tory, surrendered, 27 January 1657. [IC.ii.917]

RYDER, CLEMENT, master of the Cornelius of Wexford, 1649. [TNA.HCA13.250.250.1]

ST LAWRENCE, EDWARD, master of the Catherine of Waterford, captured by Parliamentary forces when bound from Waterford to St Malo, France, in 1646. [TNA.HCA.13.248]

SADLER, HENRY, master of the Bride of Londonderry, 1614. [UPB.66]

SADLER, RICHARD, master of the Bride of Londonderry, 1615. [UPB.86]

ST GEORGE, Captain GEORGE, an army pensioner in Ireland, a petitioner 1626. [APCE.1626.91]

ST LEGER, OLIVER, transported by Captain Bryan Fitzpatrick for service under the King of Sweden, 1630. [APCE.1630.1304]

ST LEGER, OLIVER, son and heir of Robert St Leger late of the Laugh, Queen's County, 4 March 1631. [CPRI]

SANKY, NICHOLAS, son and heir of William Sanky late of Ballilackin, King's County, 23 April 1632. [CPRI]

SARSFIELD, PETER, son and heir of Patrick Sarsfield late of Tully, County Kildare, 23 November 1632. [CPRI]

SAUNDERS, ROBERT, in Dublin, H.M. Privy Sergeant at Law, will, 1709. [DRD]

SAVAGE, ROBERT, of Ballymolen, County Down, 2 February 1631. [CPRI]

SCARDEVILLE, Reverend HENRY, Dean of Cloyn, died 3 February 1702. [Swords MI]

SCOUTE, THEODORE, from the Netherlands, a merchant in Dublin, a grant of denization in Ireland, 8 November 1638. [IPR]

SCURLOCK, BARNABY, son and heir of Walter Scurlock late of the Fraine, County Meath, 24 September 1628. [CPRI]

SCURLOCK, PATRICK, son and heir of Martin Scurlock of Rathcredan, County Dublin, of certain lands in County Meath, 1 November 1629. [CPRI]

SEADON, RANDALPH, a butcher of St Patrick Street, Dublin, took the Oath of Allegiance and Supremacy to King Charles II, on 5 April 1665.

SEAGRAVE, JOHN, in Caberagh, County Dublin, a Roman Catholic licensed to bear a sword, a case of pistols, and a gun, 30 March 1705. [HMC.Ormond.ii.477]

SEAY, RICHARD, a merchant in Waterford, 1678. [LRS.36.53]

SEDBOROUGH, JOHN, with 1000 acres in the precinct of Colinkernan, County Fermanagh, 1611. [Carew mss.1617.130]

SELLICK, DAVID, and ..... LEADER, to transport 250 Irish women, aged 12 to 45, and 300 men, aged 12 to 50, rogues, beggars and vagabonds in Youghal, Cork, Kinsale, Waterford, and Wexford, from Kinsale to New England, 25 October 1653, 28 December 1653. [IC.ii.431/443]

SERGEANT, THOMAS, in the parish of Clones, Barony of Clankelly, County Fermanagh, was killed by rebels in 1641. [PRONI.MIC.8.2]

SHAEN, Sir ARTHUR, petitioned that his lands in the Barony of Innis, County Mayo, and the parish of Termon Barry, County Roscommon, be erected into the Manor of Shaen, 11 June 1705. [TNA.SP44.240.344-5]

SHARP, THOMAS, a gentleman in Dublin, will, 1709. [DRD]

SHAW, WILLIAM, in Ballygonway, County Down, will, 1710. [DRD]

SHEA, EDMUND, granted a pass to go to Ireland 12 February 1656. [Cal.SPDom.1655.578]

SHEE, RICHARD, in Kilkenny City, a Roman Catholic licensed to bear a sword, a case of pistols, and a gun, 30 March 1705. [HMC.Ormond.ii.477]

SHEN, ROBERT, master of the Elizabeth of Derry, 1613. [UPB.56]

SHEPARD, FRANCIS, master of the Patrick of Ross, captured by Parliamentary forces when bound from New Ross to St Malo, France, in 1647. [TNA.HCA.15.2]

SHERLOCK, EDWARD, in Dublin City, a Roman Catholic licensed to bear a sword, a case of pistols, and a gun, 30 March 1705. [HMC.Ormond.ii.477]

SHERLOCK, LUCAS, born 1605, a merchant in Waterford and a passenger aboard the St Peter of Wexford, a witness before the High Court of the Admiralty of England in April 1626. [TNA.HCA13.45.265]

SHERLOCK, PAUL, surveyor of Waterford, 1617. [Carew mss.1617.178]

SHERLOCK, THOMAS, in Upper Butlerstown, County Waterford, a Roman Catholic licensed to bear a sword, a case of pistols, and a gun, 30 March 1705. [HMC.Ormond.ii.477]

SHERLOCK, WALTER, seneschal of the Laser House in Waterford, 1617. [Carew mss. 1617.178]

SHERRARD, Lady ABIGAIL, relict of Lord William Sherrard, Baron of Leitrim, probate 1657 PCC. [TNA]

SHIELD, TOBIAS, born 1608, a factor or merchant from Dublin, a witness before the High Court of the Admiralty of England in June 1641. [TNA.HCA.56.118; 57.128]

SHORTALL, JAMES, son and heir of Sir Oliver Shortall of Ballylorean, County Kilkenny, 19 July 1631. [CPRI]

SHORTALL, OLIVER, was transported by Captain Bryan Fitzpatrick for service under the King of Sweden, 1630. [APCE.1630.1304]

SHORTALL, THOMAS, born 1658 in Kilkenny, died in Landreci, French Flanders, on 19 August 1762. He was Captain of Grace's Regiment at the Siege of Limerick in 1691, and afterwards, along with the remains of the Irish army, went to France. He was made a Knight of St Louis on 6 June 1729, and a Lieutenant Colonel on 10 June 1745 after the Battle of Fontenoy. [SM.24.567]

SHUCKBURGH, RICHARD, Dean of St Saviour of Connor, to the rectory of Carrickfergus, and prebend of Killroigh, Diocese of Connor, 23 June 1628. [CPRI]

SIGINS, JOHN, master of the Catherine of Galway, from Galway to San Sebastian, Spain, and return, 1705. [TNA.SP44.390.406]

SIMCOCKS, CHARLES, born in County Cork 1661, brown hair, enlisted as a horseman of the King's Guard in 1676. [HMC.Ormonde.ii.237]

SIMPSON, GEORGE, master of the John of Strangford, captured by Parliamentary forces in 1644. [TNA.HCA.13.123]

SINNAUD, JASPER, born 1620, from Wexford, master of the Trinity, a witness before the High Court of the Admiralty of England in May 1649. [TNA.HCA.61.497/8]

SINOTT, JOHN, born 1565, from Ross in Ireland, master of the St Peter of Wexford, a witness before the High Court of the Admiralty of England in May 1626. [TNA.HCA.45.265]

SINNOTT, PATRICK, grandson and heir of Stephen Sinnott, and ward of Lisaigh McMutragh, 20 July 1632. [CPRI]

SKIDDY, JOHN, Mayor of Waterford in 1615, refused to take the Oath of Supremacy. [Carew mss.1617.184]

SLATER, JOHN, master of the Bagnall of Londonderry from Londonderry to San Sebastian, Spain, 1705. [TNA.SP44.390.388]

SLINGSBY, Captain FRANCIS, in Ballyglass, County Galway, a Roman Catholic licensed to bear a sword, a case of pistols, and a gun, 30 March 1705. [HMC.Ormond.ii.477]

SLINGSBY, HENRY, a Roman Catholic prisoner in Dublin, to be released on condition that he moved to Connaught, 6 February 1657. [IC.ii.918]

SMITH, Captain HENRY, an army pensioner in Ireland, a petitioner 1626. [APCE.1626.106]

SMITH, JOHN, master of the Robert of Kinsale, captured by Parliamentary forces when bound from Newhaven to Kinsale in 1649. [TNA.HCA.13.250i]

SMITH, Sir PERCY, born 1605, Governor of Youghal, a witness before the High Court of the Admiralty of England in March 1646. [TNA.HCA. 60.663]

SMYTHE, JOHN, master of the Gift of God of Carrickfergus, 1615. [UPB.92]

SEDGRAVE, RICHARD, son and heir of Nicholas Sedgrave late of Ballyhock, County Meath, 9 February 1632. [CPRI]

SOUTHWELL, ROBERT, a shipwright in Kinsale employed by the Commonwealth forces, 1640s. [IC.ii.p605]

SPEERES, ROBERT, master of the Gift of Strangford, from Portaferry to Wyre, 1614, later of the Speedwell of Strangford, 1614. [UPB.102/106]

SPELAN, WILLIAM, a yeoman in County Cork, 'a tory, thief or robber', to be apprehended and tried, 1692. [HMC.Ormonde.ii.449]

SPENCE, GEORGE, a brewer in Upper Combe, Dublin, will, 1709. [DRD]

SPENCER, WILLIAM, whose estate in County Cork had been destroyed, sought the estate of Hugolin Spencer an outlaw, 1697. [CTP.XLIII.72]

SPRINGATE, GULIELMA MARIA, daughter and heir of the late Sir William Springett of Langley, Kent, drew lands in the Barony of Deece, County Meath, 1659. [CSPI; 1903.73/343]

SPRINGE, EDWARD, son and heir of Walter Springe late of Killahy, County Kerry, and ward of Sir Thomas Browne, June 1632. [CPRI]

STACK, RICHARD, a yeoman in County Cork, 'a tory, thief or robber', to be apprehended and tried, 1692. [HMC.Ormonde.ii.449]

STAFFORD, Major JOHN, in Radonell, County Donegal, a Roman Catholic licensed to bear a sword, a case of pistols, and a gun, 30 March 1705. [HMC.Ormond.ii.477]

STAFFORD, PATRICK, master of the Roebuck of Wexford, was captured by Parliamentary forces when bound from Brest, France, to Wexford in 1649. [TNA.HCA.13.250.II]

STANHAWE, HENRY, was granted the lands of Clontinew, County Armagh, to be called the manor of Clontilew [sic], 1 September 1629. [CPRI]

STANLEY, CHRISTOPHER, born 1616, from Drogheda, a merchant, passenger aboard the Mayflower, a witness, April 1642. [TNA.HCA.57.456; 58.13]

STANTON, EDMUND, drew lands in the Barony of Deece, County Meath, 1659. [CSPI.1903.343]

STANYON, JAMES, armed with a snaphance, in Barony of Loughty, County Cavan, 1630. [BL.Add.MS.4770]

STAPLETON, EDWARD, son and heir of Richard Stapleton late of Fortiernagh, County Tipperary, 1 March 1631. [CPRI]

STEERES, WILLIAM, Dean of Ardfert, was appointed Bishop of Ardfert and Aghadoe in the province of Munster, 19 September 1628. [CPRI]

STEPHENS, Mr JOHN, master of the Free School in Dublin, to be dismissed, 5 November 1655. [IC.ii.750]

STEPHENSON, RICHARD, of Phiddy Island, County Cork, ward of William Stevenson {sic} and John Chetwood, 5 July 1632. [CPRI]

STOKES, HUGH, of Tawnategorman, a gentleman in the parish of Clones, Barony of Clankelly, County Fermanagh, 1641. [PRONI.MIC.8.2]

STONIFORD, JOHN, armed with a sword and pike, in Barony of Loughty, County Cavan, 1630. [BL.Add.MS.4770]

STORY, HENRY, Controller of the port of Wexford, 7 July 1629. [CPRI]

STORY, ROBERT, Controller of the port of Wexford, 7 July 1629. [CPRI]

STRAMONE, THOMAS, armed with a musket, in Barony of Loughty, County Cavan, 1630. [BL.Add.MS.4770]

STRANGE, THOMAS, granted a pass to go to Ireland 1 November 1655. [Cal.SPDom.1655.575]

STRATFORD, Captain HENRY, was granted lands in King's County to be known as the manor of Bovyne, 4 May 1629. [CPRI]

STRATTON, GRESHAM, died in Kilne Court, County Carlow, probate 1659 PCC. [TNA]

STRITCH, THOMAS, born 1615, a merchant in Limerick, a witness before the High Court of the Admiralty of England in May 1642. [TNA.HCA.58.90/105]

STRONG, CHARLES, harbinger of Waterford, 1617. [Carew mss.1617.178]

STRONG, SOLOMAN, a gentleman and receiver of the revenue and customs of Waterford, 1617. [Carew mss. 1617.178]

THE PEOPLE OF IRELAND, 1600-1699, PART FOUR

STRONGMAN, JOHN, of Ballyphilip, a juror at Blackfriars, County Waterford, 5 September 1617. [Carew mss.1617.184]

STUBBERS, Colonel, to transport 60 Irish women -vagrants, idlers and wanderers - out of Connaught to the West Indies, 26 June 1654. [IC.ii.511]

SUARY, JOHN, was appointed rector of Kilvrogan in the diocese of Cork, 2 March 1632. [CPRI]

SULLIVAN, DARBY, in Gortnecrehy, parish of Clouncagh, Barony of Conelloe, County Limerick, husband of Catherine Sullivan, will, 4 November 1708. [DRD]

SUPPLE, WILLIAM, was licenced to hold markets in Killeigh, County Cork, 11 July 1631. [CPRI]

SUTTON, CLEMENT, born 1589, from Wexford, a gentleman aboard the Arcke, a witness before the High Court of the Admiralty of England in March 1630. [TNA.HCA.48.341A/517]

SUTTON, EDMOND, of Dunnerayle, County Cork, was pardoned in Dublin on 12 December 1607. [HMC.Hastings.iv]

SUTTON, JOHN, son and heir of Richard Sutton late of Ballishop, County Wexford, 8 March 1628. [CPRI]

SUTTON, RICHARD, transported by Captain Bryan Fitzpatrick for service under the King of Sweden, 1630. [APCE.1630.1304]

SWAINTON, MICHAEL, examination, 2 September 1653. [TCD.ms829.381]

SWORDS, ROBERT, son and heir of Robert Swords alias Crowley. 13 December 1632. [CPRI]

SYMONE, MATERNE, master and merchant of the Patrick of Wexford which arrived in the River Clyde, Scotland, on 10 June 1627. [GBR]

SYMPER, THOMAS, an English Protestant, in Galway town, 1657. [HHG.appx.XXXVI]

SYNGE, SAMUEL, Dean of Kildare, died 30 November 1708, husband of Margaret, will, 1709. [DRD]

SYNOD, PATRICK, master of the Gift of God of Wexford, captured by Parliamentary forces when bound from Bilbao, Spain, to New Ross in 1642. [TNA.HCA.13.58.239]

TAAFF, Sir WILLIAM, alienated lands in the counties of Sligo and Louth to Sir Lucas Dillon, 7 March 1628. [CPRI]

TADPOLE, JOHN, born in Dublin, a blacksmith, took the Oath of Allegiance and Supremacy to King Charles II, on 12 October 1668.

TALBOT, JOHN, born 1619, a merchant from Dublin, at Nantes, France, in January 1642, a witness before the High Court of the Admiralty of England in September 1642. [TNA.HCA.58.239/240]

TALBOT, Lieutenant Colonel JOHN, in Dublin City, a Roman Catholic licensed to bear a sword, a case of pistols, and a gun, 30 March 1705. [HMC.Ormond.ii.477]

TANDY, PHILIP, drew lands in the Barony of Deece, County Meath, 1659. [CSPI. 1903.343]

TARRANT, NATHAN, born in Dublin, a stationer, took the Oath of Allegiance and Supremacy to King Charles II, on 2 October 1671.

TARREDUE, ABRAHAM, master of the Mary Fortune of Youghal, captured by Parliamentary forces in 1649. [TNA.HCA.3.232]

TAYLOR, BROCKALL, was granted lands in the Barony of Loughtee, County Cavan, to be known as the manor of Aghateeduffe alias Ballyhayes, 12 October 1629. [CPRI]

TAYLOR, Captain EDWARD, born 1646, died 14 May 1766. [Loughbrickland MI, Aghaderg]

TAYLOR, JOHN, a gentleman with 1500 acres in the precinct of Loughte, County Cavan, 1611. [Carew mss.1611.130]

TAYLOR, ROBERT, armed with a pike, in Barony of Loughty, County Cavan, 1630. [BL.Add.MS.4770]

TAYLOR, THOMAS, of Tallow, a juror at Blackfriars, County Waterford, 5 September 1617. [Carew mss.1617.184]

THE PEOPLE OF IRELAND, 1600-1699, PART FOUR

TEAGE, DANIEL, from Youghal, County Cork, died aboard the frigate Lyme at sea in state service, probate 1658 PCC. [TNA]

TEAT, NATHANIELL, armed with a sword and pike, in Barony of Loughty, County Cavan, 1630. [BL.Add.MS.4770]

TEELING, MICHAEL, merchant in Wexford, 1647. [TNA.HCA.15.2]

TEMPLER, EDWARD, born in Waterford 1651, brown hair, enlisted as a horseman of the King's Guard in 1669. [HMC.Ormonde.ii.237]

TENNANT, JOHN, master of the Neptune of Sligo, from Ireland to San Sebastian, Spain, and return, 1705. [TNA.SP44.392.71]

TENNISON, HENRY, in Dublin, to build the Queen's dog kennel there, 20 May 1706. [TNA.SO.1.15.323]

TERRELL, WALTER, born 1600, a merchant in Dublin, a witness before the High Court of the Admiralty of England in December 1641. [TNA.HCA.57.321]

THEAKER, THOMAS, merchant burgess of Belfast, died 12 March 1660, probate 24 November 1691.

THEAKER, SAMPSON, of the Church of Ireland, a gentleman and a burgess of Belfast from 1681 to 1692. [BMF]

THEOBALD, SAMPSON, was appointed Summonister of the Court of Exchequer on 3 September 1629. [CPRI]

THETFORD, FRANCIS, of the Church of Ireland, a merchant and a burgess of Belfast from 1665 to 1690. [BMF]

THETFORD, HENRY, of the Church of Ireland, a joiner and a burgess of Belfast from 1677 to 1678. [BMF]

THOMAS, DANIEL, in Bellamoe, County Galway, probate 1659 PCC. [TNA]

THOMAS, DAVID, rector of Castlecor and vicar of Portneshangan and Raconnell, in the Diocese of Meath, 22 July 1631. [CPRI]

THOMAS, WALTER, merchant in Downpatrick, aboard the Henry of Carlingford from Carlingford to Downpatrick in 1615. [UPB.105]

THOMASIN, THOMAS, granted a pass to go to Ireland 16 November 1655. [Cal.SPDom.1655.575]

THOMPSON, JOHN, granted a pass to go to Ireland 29 April 1656. [Cal.SPDom.1655.581]

THOMPSON, LEWIS, Dutch or Flemish, of the Church of Ireland, a merchant and a burgess of Belfast from 1678 to 1708. [BMF]

THORNTON, TRISTRAM, born in Coleraine 1657, grey hair, enlisted as a horseman of the King's Guard in 1675. [HMC.Ormonde.ii.237]

THORP, JOHN, in Barony of Loughty, County Cavan, 1630. [BL.Add.MS.4770]

THORP, JOHN, born 1609, a sailor from Dublin, a witness before the High Court of the Admiralty of England in April 1643. [TNA.HCA.58.443/510]

THORP, WILLIAM, in Barony of Loughty, County Cavan, 1630. [BL.Add.MS.4770]

THROGMORTON, Sir BAYNHAM, granted a pass to go to Ireland 5 December 1655. [Cal.SPDom.1655.575]

THYNNE, THOMAS, merchant in London, drew lands in the Barony of Upper Iveagh, County Down, 1659. [CSPI; 1903.343]

TICHBORNE, Sir HENRY, of Bewley, County Louth, drew lands in the south east quarter of the Barony of Lecale, County Down, 1659. [CSPI; 1903.29/342]

TIGH, RICHARD, an alderman of Dublin, 1673. [SPDom.1673.527]

TILBY, ABRAHAM, born in Limerick 1644, brown hair, enlisted as a horseman of the King's Guard in 1674. [HMC.Ormonde.ii.237]

TINTE, WILLIAM, transported by Captain Bryan Fitzpatrick for service under the King of Sweden, 1630. [APCE.1630.1304]

TITCHBOURNE, HENRY, was granted lands in the Barony of Clogher and in the barony of Strabane, 7 July 1629. [CPRI]

TOBIN, ROBERT, transported by Captain Bryan Fitzpatrick for service under the King of Sweden, 1630. [APCE.1630.1304]

TOBINE, ROBERT JAMES, transported by Captain Bryan Fitzpatrick for service under the King of Sweden, 1630. [APCE.1630.1304]

TOBIN, THOMAS, son and heir of Richard Tobin late of Pullcaple, County Tipperary, 7 February 1631. [CPRI]

TODD, JAMES, born 1646, died 13 December 1704. [Loughbrickland MI, Aghaderg]

TOLLCHARD, GEORGE, a soldier in Baltimore, County Cork, was pardoned in Dublin on 18 January 1608. [HMC. Hastings.iv.29]

TOLLER, JOHN, a yeoman in County Cork, 'a tory, thief or robber', to be apprehended and tried, 1692. [HMC.Ormonde.ii.449]

TOMSON, JOSEPH, born 1699, died 27 April 1718. [Seapatrick MI]

TOOLE, CARBRY OGE MCCAN, a native who was granted land in the Precinct of Oriel, 1611. [Carew mss]

TOOLE, FRANCIS, in Dublin City, a Roman Catholic licensed to bear a sword, a case of pistols, and a gun, 30 March 1705. [HMC.Ormond.ii.477]

TOOLEY, JOHN, of the Church of Ireland, an apothecary and a burgess of Belfast from 1682 to 1687. [BMF]

TOOMEY, THOMAS, in Kinsale, 1635. [IC.ii.p.604]

TRANT, RICHARD, a gentleman from Dingle, a soldier who settled in Spain during 1603. [AGS.E.leg.1745]

TRAVERS, PETER, a merchant in Bridge Street, Dublin, 1673. [SPDom.1673.527]

TRAVERS, THOMAS, in Burgess, County Tipperary, a Roman Catholic licensed to bear a gun, 30 March 1705. [HMC.Ormond.ii.477]

TREVILION, GEORGE, with 4000 acres in Wexford, 1616. [Carew mss. 1616.168]

TROW, RICHARD, granted a pass to go to Ireland 13 March 1656. [Cal.SPDom.1655.579]

TULLY, THOMAS, born 1622, a merchant in Galway, a witness before the High Court of the Admiralty of England in November 1644. [TNA.HCA13.59.565]

TURNER, CHARLES, master of the privateer Mary Conception of Wexford, 1648-1649. [TNA.HCA.13.251.i]

TURNER, JOHN, examination, 23 March 1644. [TCD.ms830.146]

TURNER, RICHARD, drew lands in the Barony of Deece, County Meath, 1659. [CSPI; 1903.343]

TURNER, THOMAS, drew lands in the Barony of Deece, County Meath, 1659. [CSPI.1903.343]

TURNER, WALTER, born 1591, from Wexford, master of the St George, a witness before the High Court of the Admiralty of England in October 1634. [TNA.HCA13.51.18]

TURVINE, WILLIAM, a gentleman, with 2000 acres in the precinct of Clogher, County Tyrone, 1611. [Carew mss. 1611.130]

TWIGG, CHARLES, born in Cavan 1635, brown hair, enlisted as a horseman of the King's Guard in 1666. [HMC.Ormonde.ii.237]

UNEDALL, WILLIAM, and Sir JOHN STANHOPE, were granted 2627 acres in the Barony of Omey, County Tyrone, to be known as the manor of Hastings, 13 April 1631. [CPRI]

USHER, PATRICK, in Dublin City, a Roman Catholic licensed to bear a sword, a case of pistols, and a gun, 30 March 1705. [HMC.Ormond.ii.477]

VAN DALE, JOHN, from Brabant, Flanders, a grant of denization in Ireland, 7 June 1605. [IPR]

VAN DE RYDER, CLEMENT, master of the Cornelius of Wexford, 1649. [TNA.HCA.13.250.I]

VAN DER BEGGE, JAMES, from the Netherlands, a grant of denization in Ireland, 22 March 1639. [IPR]

THE PEOPLE OF IRELAND, 1600-1699, PART FOUR

VAN DER MARCHE, ANTONIO, master of the Mary of Antrim, 1649. [TNA.HCA.13.250/1]

VAN DER SHUREN, NICATIUS, from the Netherlands, a grant of denization in Ireland, 27 February 1635. [IPR]

VAN DER VOORT, ABRAHAM, from the Netherlands, a grant of denization in Ireland, 27 February 1635. [IPR]

VAN DER VOORT, JOHN, from the Netherlands, a grant of denization in Ireland, 27 February 1635. [IPR]

VAN DUNDREIGHT, GERROT VAN ASPEREN, from the Netherlands, a grant of denization in Ireland, 29 January 1620. [IPR]

VAN HOVEN, GERRARD, from Amsterdam, Holland, a grant of denization in Ireland, 5 March 1646. [Patent Roll, 21 Car 1.14]

VAN VOOREN, DANIEL, master of the St John of Waterford, 1648. [TNA.HCA13.250]

VAUGHAN, HECTOR, in Knocknamease, King's County, will, 1710. [DVD]

VEALE, JOHN, son and heir of Henry Veale late of Skarte, County Waterford, 24 July 1632. [CPRI]

VELDON, PATRICK, master of the Mary Ann of Dublin, from Ireland to Catalonia, in December 1705. [TNA.SP42.119/193]

VERHOVEN, GERALD, from Antwerp, Flander, a grant of denization in Ireland, 18 June 1605. [IPR]

VERHOVEN, JOHN, alias John de la Grange, from Brabant, Flanders, a grant of denization in Ireland, 7 June 1705. [IPR]

VINCENT, THOMAS, of Peckham, Surrey, drew lands in the Barony of Deece, County Meath, 1659. [CSPI; 1903.343]

VINES, STEPHEN, a merchant in Ireland, co-owner of the Hopewell of Galway trading with Barbados pre 1668. [ActsPCCol.1668.744]

WADDING, PATRICK, master of the privateer St John of Wexford, 1649. [TNA.HCA.15.2]

THE PEOPLE OF IRELAND, 1600-1699, PART FOUR

WADDING, RICHARD, surveyor of Waterford, 1617. [Carew mss. 1617.178]

WADDING, WILLIAM, master of the 40 ton privateer Mary and Joseph of Wexford, 1648-1649. [TNA.HCA.30.855.335; 13.250/1]

WAGSTAFFE, EDMUND, drew lands in the Barony of Upper Iveagh, County Down, 1659. [CSPI.1903.343]

WALCOT, THOMAS, of the Church of Ireland, a gentleman and a burgess of Belfast from 1660 to 1690. [BMF]

WALDRON, RICHARD, a gentleman with 2000 acres in the precinct of Loughte, County Cavan, 1611. [Carew mss.1611.130]

WALE, WILLIAM, son and heir of Gerald Wale late of Cwilnymucky, County Waterford, 13 July 1632. [CPRI]

WALLE, EDMOND, transported by Captain Bryan Fitzpatrick for service under the King of Sweden, 1630. [APCE.1630.1304]

WALL, EDWARD, born in Catherlough 1652, flaxen hair, enlisted as a horseman of the King's Guard in 1674. [HMC.Ormonde.ii.237]

WALL, EDY, cousin and heir of Richard Wall late of Palmerstown, County Carlow, 1 August 1631. [CPRI]

WALL, MICHAEL, born in Waterford 1651, brown hair, enlisted as a horseman of the King's Guard in 1673. [HMC.Ormonde.ii.237]

WALLACE, NICHOLAS, master of the James of Dublin, from Dublin to Bilbao, Spain, in 1705. [TNA.SP44.390.323]

WALSH, JOHN, yeoman in Cram, County Limerick, was pardoned in Dublin on 23 July 1608. [HMC.Hastings.iv.32]

WALSH, JOHN, of Ballyawly, Dublin, 1611. [Carew mss]

WALSH, JOHN, late in Dublin, later in Shagnogh, County Dublin, a Roman Catholic licensed to bear a sword, a case of pistols, and a gun, 30 March 1705. [HMC.Ormond.ii.477]

WALSH, alias ROURK, MARY, a widow in Dublin, will, 1709. [DRD]

WALSH, PETER, a priest in Flanders, permitted to recruit 4000 Irishmen to serve the King of Spain, 26 May 1653. [IC.ii.343]

WALSH, PHILIP, master of the sloop Dragon, from Cork to Bilbao, Spain, 1705. [TNA.SP44.392.70]

WALSH, THOMAS, son and heir of Nicholas Walsh late of Bushe, County Wexford, 8 March 1632. [CPRI]

WALSH, THOMAS, in County Waterford, a petition, 23 May 1655. [IC.ii.680]

WARD, EDWARD, a gentleman with 1000 acres in the precinct of Colinkernan, County Fermanagh, 1611. [Carew mss.1617.130]

WARING, THOMAS, of the Church of Ireland, a tanner and a merchant burgess of Belfast from 1652 to 1665, [BMF], died 23 November 1665, probate 2 January 1666.

WARING, WILLIAM, of the Church of Ireland, a tanner & merchant and a burgess of Belfast from 1660 to 1675. [BMF]

WARRE, WALTER, was appointed to the office of Customer, Collector and Receiver of His Majesty's customs, imposts, and subsidies in the port of Dinglecuish, County Kerry, on 22 June 1629. [CPRI]

WARREN, ALEXANDER, resident of Galway, 11 April 1652. [HHG, appx.xxxii]

WARREN, JOHN, born in Clantarfe, a cooper, took the Oath of Allegiance and Supremacy to King Charles II, on 26 May 1670.

WARREN, Captain MICHAEL, in Warrenstown, County Meath, a Roman Catholic licensed to bear a sword, a case of pistols, and a gun, 30 March 1705. [HMC.Ormond.ii.477]

WARREN, THOMAS, in Corduffe, County Dublin, a Roman Catholic licensed to bear a sword, a case of pistols, and a gun, 30 March 1705. [HMC.Ormond.ii.477]

WARREN, WILLIAM, of Warrentown, County Meath, 24 September 1629. [CPRI]

WATERHOUSE, THOMAS, fishmonger in London, drew lands in the Barony of Deece, County Meath, 1659. [CSPI.1903.343]

WATTS, WILLIAM, a merchant in Dublin, trading with Antwerp and Ostend, Flanders, in 1666, he along with Francis Kniffe and Alexander Deschodt, merchants in Antwerp, loaded the St Francis of Antwerp with merchandise bound for Ireland which was wrecked off Portpatrick, Scotland. [NAS.RH9.5.31]

WEBB, WILLIAM and THOMAS WHITMORE, were given the monopoly of all royal mines and mineral works in Munster for 21 years, 8 June 1631. [CPRI]

WEBSTER, RICHARD, un-armed, in Barony of Loughty, County Cavan, 1630. [BL.Add.MS.4770]

WELCH, JAMES, born 1602, a merchant in Dublin, a witness before the High Court of the Admiralty of England in July 1625. [TNA.HCA13.45.23]

WELLS, BLANERHASSET, an English Protestant, in Galway town, 1657. [HHG.appx.XXXVI]

WENHAM, Sir RICHARD, was created Baron Wenham of Kilmainham, County Dublin, also Viscount Wenman of Tuam on 30 July 1628. [CPRI]

WENMAN, THOMAS, was appointed to the office of Provost Marshal of Munster, on 7 July 1629. [CPRI]

WEST, REVELL, master of the Margaret of Londonderry, from Ireland to Bilbao, Spain, 1705. [TNA.SP44.392.73/372]

WESTENRA, ARNOLD, from Campen, Overissell, Holland, a grant of denizisation in Ireland, [IPR.19-24 Car i.14]

WESTENRA, DERICKE, born in Campen, Overissillis, Holland, a merchant in Ireland, and his sons Peter and Warner, grants of naturalization, 22 November 1655. [Patent Roll, Commonwealth, 1.3/29]; 1662, [14-15 Car ii]

WESTENRA, WARNER, from Harlem, Holland, a grant of denization in Ireland, 22 November 1655. [Patent Roll, Commonwealth.1.3/29]; a merchant, a grant of naturalization, 1662. [14-15 Car ii]

West Meath, the Earl of, a Roman Catholic licensed to bear a sword, a case of pistols, and a gun, 30 March 1705. [HMC.Ormond.ii.477]

WHARTON, Sir THOMAS, drew lands in the Barony of Deece, County Meath, 1659. [CSPI.1903.343]

WHETCOMBE, TRISTRAM, burgess of Kinsale, County Cork, probate 1659 PCC. [TNA]

WHISTLER, RALPH, was appointed Customs Controller of the port of Drogheda on 2 November 1629. [CPRI]

WHISTLER, RALPH, was licenced to hold markets in the town of Magherafelt, County Londonderry, 22 February 1631. [CPRI]

WHITAKER, THOMAS, was appointed joint Customs Controller of the port of Drogheda on 2 July 1629. [CPRI]

WHITBY, Captain MARCUS, in Fermoy, Cork, probate 1660 PCC. [TNA]

WHITE, JAMES, water bailiff of Waterford, 1617. [Carew mss. 1617.178]

WHITE, JAMES, master of the Joseph of Dublin from Dublin to Bilbao, Spain, 1705; from Bilbao to Dublin, 1706. [TNA.SP44.393.20; SP63.366.63]

WHITE, Colonel , in Rahagoone, County Limerick, a Roman Catholic licensed to bear a sword, a case of pistols, and a gun, 30 March 1705. [HMC.Ormond.ii.477]

WHITE, MICHAEL, merchant in Carrickfergus, aboard the Sunday of Ardglass, at Carrickfergus in 1614; 1615. [UPB.94/95]

WHITE, PIERCE, master of the Mary of Wexford, captured by Parliamentary forces when bound from Wexford to St Malo, France, in 1648. [TNA.HCA.30.855.245]

WHITE, RICHARD, master of the John of Drogheda, captured by Parliamentary forces in 1642. [TNA.HCA.13.58.158]

WHITE, THOMAS, gentleman, churchwarden of Christchurch, Waterford, 1617. [Carew.1617.178]

WHITE, THOMAS, surveyor of Waterford, 1617. [Carew mss.1617.178]

WHITE, WILLIAM, born 1617, a seaman in Wexford, a witness before the High Court of the Admiralty of England in June 1644. [TNA.HCA13.59.300]

WHITE, WILLIAM, master and merchant of the <u>Katherine of Wexford</u>, which arrived in the River Clyde, Scotland, in June 1627. [GBR]

WHITNEY, ROBERT, of Syan, Queen's County, 1611. [Carew mss]

WHITTY, PATRICK, born 1612, a mariner from Galway aboard the <u>St George of Galway</u>, a witness before the High Court of the Admiralty of England in September 1633. [TNA.HCA13.50.408]

WHITTY, RICHARD, son and heir of Walter Whitty late of Balliteig, County Wexford, 20 July 1632. [CPRI]

WIGGINS, JESSE, in Barony of Loughty, County Cavan, 1630. [BL.Add.MS.4770]

WILCOX, JEFFREY, in Barony of Loughty, County Cavan, 1630. [BL.Add.MS.4770]

WILEY, NATHANIEL, aged 106, died at Clogh near Ballymena on 19 February 1758. 'He was petty constable of Ballymena when King James VII's army marched in 1689 to besiege Londonderry. He used to say, he served two kings in one day; King William in the forenoon, out of love; and King James in the afternoon out of fear'. [SM.20.110]

WILKS, THOMAS, master of the <u>Marcelia of Dublin</u>, a galley, from Ireland to Barcelona, Spain, in December 1705. [TNA.SP42.119.193]

WILLIAMS, GRIETGE, from Ireland, married Hendry Hendry, a soldier from Orkney, Scotland, in Rotterdam, the Netherlands, on 26 March 1606. [Rotterdam Marriage Register]

WILLIAMS, THOMAS, an English Protestant, in Galway town, 1657. [HHG.appx.XXXVI]

THE PEOPLE OF IRELAND, 1600-1699, PART FOUR

WILLIAMS, WALTER, born 1623, from Kinsale, a mariner aboard the Love of London, a witness before the High Court of the Admiralty of England in January 1645. [TNA.HCA13.59.624]

WILLIAMSON, JOHN, born in Conner, County Antrim, a tailor, took the Oath of Allegiance and Supremacy to King Charles II, on 15 December 1668.

WILLOUGHBY, FRANCIS, with 2000 acres in the precinct of Clogher, County Tyrone, 1611. [Carew mss. 1611.130]

WILLSON, THOMAS, of Mullaghglass, yeoman in County Armagh, was proclaimed a traitor and rebel on 14 December 1674. [HMC.Ormonde.ii.342/3]

WILSON, WILLIAM, with 2000 acres in the precinct of Liffer, County Donegal, 1611. [Carew mss. 1611.130]

WILSON, WILLIAM, master of the Henry of Carlingford, 1615. [UPB. 104]

WINDSOR, FRANCIS, a gentleman from the Netherlands, a grant of denization in Ireland, 9 June 1626. [IPR]

WINGFIELD, Sir RICHARD, with 1000 acres in Wexford, 1616. [Carew mss.1616.168]

WINGFIELD, ..., 'a kinsman of the Marshals', with 1000 acres in Wexford, 1616. [Carew mss.1616.168]

WIRRELL, Sir HUGH, a gentleman with 1500 acres in the precinct of Loughte, County Cavan, 1611. [Carew mss.1611.130]

WISE, JAMES, master of the Pelican of Coleraine, 1613, and of the Mathew and Margaret of Coleraine, 1613. [UPB.60/62]

WISNAME, SYMOND, in Barony of Loughty, County Cavan, 1630. [BL.Add.MS.4770]

WITTON, RICHARD, in Barony of Loughty, County Cavan, 1630. [BL.Add.MS.4770]

WOGAN, Captain JOHN, an army pensioner in Ireland, a petitioner 1626. [APCE.1626.97]

THE PEOPLE OF IRELAND, 1600-1699, PART FOUR

WOGAN, THOMAS, master of the Mary of Dublin, from Youghall to Bilbao, Spain, 1705. [TNA.SP44.390.350]

WOLFE, JAMES, merchant in Limerick City, was granted land in County Limerick, 23 March 1628. [CPRI]

WOOD, JEREMIAH, yeoman in Epping, Essex, drew lands in the Barony of Deece, County Meath, 1659. [CSPI.1903.343]

WOOD, JOHN, wool-comber of St Mary Matfellon, Middlesex, drew lands in the Barony of Deece, County Meath, 1659. [CSPI.1903.343]

WOOD, MARY, drew lands in the Barony of Upper Iveagh, County Down, 1659. [CSPI.1903.343]

WOODLOCKE, JAMES, a gentleman and Receiver of the Revenue and Customs of Waterford, 1617. [Carew mss. 1617.178]

WOODRUFFE, GEORGE, master of the Bride of Londonderry, 1615. [UPB.32]

WOOGAN, Lieutenant Colonel JOHN, in Rathcoffy, County Kildare, a Roman Catholic licensed to bear a sword, a case of pistols, and a gun, 30 March 1705. [HMC.Ormond.ii.477]

WOORALL, Sir HUGH, with 1000 acres in the precinct of Clancally, County Fermanagh, 1611. [Carew mss. 1611.130]

WRAY, WILLIAM, in Fore, County Donegal, husband of Angel, will, 1710. [DRD]

WRIGHT, JOHN, granted a pass to go to Ireland 27 March 1656. [Cal.SPDom.1655.580]

WYBRANTS, DANIEL, senior, an Alderman of Dublin, a Dutch subject, was naturalised in Ireland, along with his wife Elizabeth and children including his sons Daniel junior, Peter, and Henry, however Daniel sr. died in Holland before 1673. [SPDom.1673.500]

WYE, GILBERT, of the Church of Ireland, a burgess of Belfast from 1662 to 1680. [BMF]

YOUNG, CHARLES, son and heir of Sir James Young late of Castlebarne, County Longford, and ward of Patrick Young, 22 November 1632. [CPRI]

REFERENCES

ADHG=		Archives departmentales de la Haute Garonne, France
AGS	=	Archivo General de Simancas, Spain
AHN	=	Archivo Historico Nacional, Spain
AMT	=	Archives municipals de Toulouse, France
APCE	=	Acts of the Privy Council of England, series
BL	=	British Library, London
BLO	=	Bodleian Library, Oxford
BMF	=	Belfast Merchant Families in the 17th Century, J. Agnew, [Dublin, 1996]
CA	=	Cork Archives, Ireland
Carew=		Calendar of the Carew Manuscripts in Lambeth Palace
CLRO =		City of London Record Office
CPRI	=	Calendar of Patent Rolls, Ireland
CSPI	=	Calendar of State Papers, Ireland, series
CTP	=	Calendar of Treasury Papers, series
DRD	=	Dublin Register of Deeds
EMA	=	List of Emigrant Ministers to America, 1690-1811, G. Fothergill, [London, 1904]
GAR	=	Rotterdam Archives, Netherlands

GBR	=	Glasgow Burgh Records
HHG	=	History of Galway, J. Hardiman, [Dublin, 1820]
HMC	=	Historical Manuscript Commission, London
IC	=	Ireland under the Commonwealth, [Manchester, 1913]
IPR	=	Irish Patent Rolls, series
LRO	=	Liverpool Record Office
LRS	=	London Record Society, London
MI	=	Monumental Inscription
NAS	=	National Archives of Scotland, Edinburgh
PCC	=	Prerogative Court of Canterbury
PL	=	Pilgrims and other people from the British Isles in Leiden, 1576-1640. [Isle of Man, 1989]
PRONI		Public Record Office, Northern Ireland, Belfast
RAB	=	Rijksarchief Brugge, Belgium
RPCS	=	Register of the Privy Council of Scotland
SAA	=	Stadsarchief Antwerpen, Belgium
SM	=	Scots Magazine, series, Edinburgh
SPAWI	=	State Papers, America and the West Indies, series
SPDom		State Papers, Domestic, series
TCD	=	Trinity College, Dublin
TNA	=	The National Archives, London
UPB	=	The Ulster Port Books, 1612-1615. [Belfast, 2012]
VaGaz	=	Virginia Gazette, series

www.ingramcontent.com/pod-product-compliance
Lightning Source LLC
Chambersburg PA
CBHW070920180426
43192CB00038B/2095